Never Personal Always Purpose Presents

The Power of Purpose

Monique Turner

I want to thank God for his favor, grace and mercy. My beautiful wife, Tiffany Turner, who's been with me through this transition from the streets to the boardroom. I wouldn't be complete without her; she has played a big role in helping me to get this book together. It's a blessing to have a partner that you can share every moment with. She's more than my wife; she's my everything and beyond.

I love each of my kings that God blessed me with, Anthony Jr, Bryce, Julian and Dante Jr. They give me life, they give me a reason to go hard each day. I pray that God keeps them covered and in covenant with him. I love how they each have the ambition to be the best at all that they do. Anthony serves at a young age; it's amazing to me how he walks in purpose and doesn't even know it. His mission is to help and give to those less fortunate. Bryce will be our Engineer; he will create the blueprint for our community center. He's super smart, talented and could do anything he puts his mind to. Julian is passionate about music and dancing. I can see him being a computer specialist, gamer or musician of some kind. Dante Jr's passion is basketball. That boy has been shooting a ball since he could walk, and I know that he will grow up and have something to do with sports.

I'm someone that can be hard to work with at times because I'm a visionary and always coming up with a new task. Kanika Jenkins has been with me every step of the way, and I'm really thankful for her; she has edited all my books. She's more than a business partner; she's my friend. Over the years, we have created so many programs to help youth overcome the obstacles that life sends our way. I'm enjoying this journey that God has us on together, and she's a big part of the team.

I love each of my siblings, nieces, nephews, cousins, and all my family (friends + family). I pray that God blesses our family and keeps us all in one accord as we go through this journey of life. Mommy and Daddy, thank you for loving me and teaching me everything I know. I wish you could be here with me, and I can feel your presence surrounding me, but to hear your voice and have your support physically is something I wish I had every day.

I want to give a special thank you to all my readers and supporters. Y'all give me the courage to keep going. I appreciate all the support that you've given me over the years, this is the third book, but we are just getting started.

Chapter 1:

Looking into the mirror, taking off the mask and getting real with yourself

Being an adult doesn't mean you know who you are. So many people wear a mask to cover up the person they don't want to see or be. This can happen for multiple reasons: trauma that may have occurred at a young age, believing negative things about yourself (you're ugly, small, big, stupid, a mistake, disgrace), or trying to avoid unresolved issues from your childhood. I think back when I was a child, and my parents didn't acknowledge any of the events that were taking place that I believe had traumatizing effects on my siblings and me.

Before I was a teenager, my house was raided by police, and the door was kicked in. I also witnessed my parents' drug use in the house. My father was the man on the block who supplied all the dealers that got high with drugs for their personal use. Though this would be considered inappropriate by many, this was all part of my normal daily life. I had been laid down by police time and time again because of people snitching on my dad about the drug dealing. Interestingly, they never found anything, so as soon as the police left, life was back to normal. I can remember watching my dad flush the drugs down the toilet when he heard them banging at our door. One time, they took my uncle to jail, but he was later released. I don't know if he bailed out, or they let him out. My parents never sat us down after any of those raids to explain what happened, nor ask us how we were feeling. On the flip side of this, we had everyone outside witnessing what was happening in our apartment; it is the projects, so everyone is right there, and they know exactly what just went down. Our house was a revolving door. As soon as it closed, it was being opened back up. If it wasn't the police raiding, it was someone coming to buy from my dad or hang out with him talking about sports.

What's funny is, as I look back now, I realize that my parents wore masks. My dad worked for a furniture company. He was a really good business man-I'm sure that's where I get my business mind from. Before I was born, he was the manager of a car wash, and he gave my uncle his first job. He was also all about helping people; he would always see the good in someone. When I had my son, he bought us a restaurant and named it the Turner Family Kitchen. We didn't have it long because he traveled for work, and nobody knew how to run the business like him. When my father went on business trips, he would get dressed up so nice. He looked like 'New Money.' He was so good at being a leader; he ran the whole San Francisco showroom. I was so happy when he was in San Francisco because this meant that he was staying home instead of leaving. When he would be home, he wore the same sweat pants all the time. He never cared to get dressed, and he didn't care about anyone's opinion of him. When he was home, he was the drug dealer and the shit talker. The people he worked for never knew of his other life, and he maintained this facade with them for over 10 years.

The next contrast within my father was the high him and the sober him. I was partial to the high him. When he was high, he would always say Yes, especially if he was in the moment. He was also more open when he was high. There were times when I would go into the kitchen and talk to him, and he would tell me everything about the drug dealing business. When he would be sober, he wasn't having it. He was so mean and a strict disciplinarian. We had to be in the house by 6pm, couldn't leave the first court, couldn't have company and the list goes on. For us kids, it was all bad, but it was really all good. It was this part of him that was the businessman, the head of his household, making sure his kids were doing what we were supposed to do.

Going down memory lane about my parents and reflecting on my childhood really helps me understand why I am the way I am. I wonder what other masks my daddy wore and why he was the way he was. My grandma always has great stories about my dad, and I'm thankful for that. I wish that I could talk to my parents and hear what they have to say about some of the events from my childhood that I see as key in my development. I know now that they were the sacrifice for me to get my life right, and I will continue the legacy and make them proud.

Let's talk about my mom's mask. She was so sweet and loving. She fed everybody and would take kids from the neighborhood on family outings with us. She loved to party and have a good time. This was the person that everyone saw, including my dad. But this was not the person she was when my dad was out of state for work. When my father was gone, my mother was wild. My mom would go out and drink and then come home acting sweet. This was just phase one. Soon after coming home and playing nice, things quickly escalated to World War 2. She would hit us, slam things, break things and then need a bucket to throw up in. Then came all the "I Love You's." This would frustrate me so much. It made me resent my mom. I really hated when my dad would leave and always felt that I loved him more than I loved my mom. Like my dad, she had two sides, and this was confusing and frustrating for me. When my dad was gone, she was the cool mom because she let me do things my dad wouldn't, like staying home from school, staying outside late, having company-the freedom we didn't have with my dad. But when she turned into the drinker, the dynamic was so different, I didn't want her around me or my friends. They all loved her, they loved to be around my mom, but I didn't, not when she was like that. Don't get me wrong; I loved my mom; she was the best. I didn't like her behavior and because of that, and the fact that I had not lived enough to understand the reasons behind such behavior, my perception of her was clouded.

As I got older, I picked up all the same habits that my parents had shown me. At the age of 10, I was outside selling drugs instead of playing sports, riding bikes, and having balloon fights, things a ten-year-old needed to be doing. Don't get me wrong, I was still a kid playing games and having fun, but making money was my priority. I was so good at what I was doing that my parents never caught me. People would tell on me, but I would lie and make something up. So, as you can see, the mask for me came on at a young age, and I didn't even realize that I was wearing a mask as a kid. It wasn't until I got in my 30s that I really began to understand who Monique really was and started to reflect on the things that I encountered as a child. When we avoid dealing with our issues, we set ourselves up for much larger issues later. It may even feel good like it's all behind you until something comes up that triggers those emotions again. When past emotions are triggered, either we face them head-on or feel overwhelmed and find ourselves worse off than we were before. It's not good to leave our emotions unchecked. Looking in the mirror is only beneficial when we can prevent our fear from controlling our perceptions. The mask will remain on if you don't face the past, and you will never know who you really are. To understand your authentic self, you must face the person from the past, the little you, the you that is hard to remember, the you that nobody knows.

There isn't any way around the face in the mirror. You might be able to mask that person for years, but the truth of the matter is, the mask was developed to protect you. However, it is really causing you to suffer as you are getting farther and farther away from your true self.

Think about this: what do you see when you look in the mirror? Some of us don't even realize that we wear a mask because everything is so routine. Your coverup has become your normal, and even though you don't see it, you put on a mask every day as your way of coping. Once you're used to putting the mask on, it makes it hard to take it off, but anything is possible if you put your mind to it. The key is understanding why you put the mask on in the first place. When you find your why, you can begin to have a better understanding of what steps need to be taken moving forward to remove it and become comfortable with the person you see.

Let's work through a few steps together. These are a few questions that you will want to write down; this way, you can answer clearly and be able to go back and reflect on your answers.

When you were in grade school, did you have lots of friends?

Were you a social person?

Were you bullied, or were you the bully?

What kind of relationship did you have with your parents and /or siblings?

Did your parents/guardian allow you to do things you enjoyed?

Did your parents/guardian allow you to explore your hobbies?

What was the most challenging thing for you since birth and becoming a teenager?

These are some very important questions, which will help you see when the mask became part of your life. Then you will see when you began to seek the mask as your coping mechanism. This is very important for the process of removing the mask. Sometimes, we don't want to face our past because of the different challenges that we've faced along the way and addressing these wounds might not be your strong point. Where are you in your life right now? It can cause more harm than good because of your way of thinking. I understand that first hand and, therefore, I've included so much about my life, so you can see that I am only telling you what I know and that I've worn a mask since a child. Had God not given me the vision to write this book, I might not have ever realized just how much I've run from myself and kept so many secrets. Looking back, I can see that I had a great childhood, considering the circumstances I lived in. However, this is a difficult thing to do because growing up, we may not identify our experiences as good or bad—they are just normal, until we learn otherwise. Sometimes, when we have childhood experiences that we identify as unpleasant, we suppress the memories in the hopes of forgetting or pretend as if these things didn't happen, and eventually, they turn into forgotten memories.

I don't know where I would be mentally if it weren't for God giving me the vision to found a nonprofit, focusing on strengthening our community, beginning with its foundation- family and children, in 2010. Speaking to youth and young adults is my outlet, and I was blessed to be able to start my organization in 2013. It is through these works that I've been able to overcome a lot of the issues I've buried away and suffered as a child. I can see myself through the youth I work with. They've given me life over the past few years. The Lord knew who and what I needed, and I am grateful that I was obedient and followed his path. It took me thirty-three years before I completely surrendered, but when I finally did, it was the beginning of the transformation and this journey I'm on today. It was at this point that I was able to see not only the fact that I had been wearing a mask but that it was soon to be removed.

I wish I had my parents to speak with about it; I need answers that I will never get. Now, the only answers I get are the ones in my head. I allowed the streets to keep me from who I cherish today, my family. I think it's very important to speak with your parents or siblings about your childhood traumas. This process can't be skipped because your freedom depends on it. When I say your freedom, I'm talking about your spirit being free from all the pain that you've kept bottled up inside over the years. I never talked about all the bad things that happened to me as a kid. I didn't remember a lot of it, and the more time that went on, the more it became a distant memory. It wasn't until my wife and students came into my life that I began to reflect on my life.

Because I was hurt and nobody protected me, I created another person in my mind. My family and friends knew of this person, but they figured it was just a phase, but she was real, and she was my protector. She was the only person that really knew the real me; she knew me better than I knew me. Parents assume that when kids create imaginary friends that it's all for fun, but sometimes, it can be something serious going on like it was for me. Sometimes, it is the wall that is put up to protect the child from harm outside of his or her control. I used to think I was in control of my friend

Mone.' I wasn't in control of her; she was in control of me; she had my mind. I would to go to school and tell the teacher that my name wasn't Monique, it was Mone.' I would tell her that Monique was my twin sister. The teacher thought I was just being defiant. Sometimes, she would call my mom but that didn't do anything because my mom knew I would use the name Mone.' Throughout grade school, nobody paid attention to the signs of something being wrong with me.

Was it normal for a child to go to school and pretend to be someone else? Did teachers deal with this often? Why wasn't a parent conference ever held regarding my behavior? These are all the things I think about now, and I wonder how my life would've been different had someone tried to help me with the many voices in my head.

Fast forward to the teenager in me and what it was like when I went through puberty. As I find myself reflecting on Monique and Mone' and how they showed up during this time, I ask myself: Was it easy for me to get a girl/boyfriends? Did I have friends when I was in high school? What did I do for fun? What was the worst part of being a teenager? What was the best part about being a teenager?

Puberty is a big deal for teenagers. The things that we experience during puberty are the things that play a role in how we mature into our teenage years. Our bodies are changing to prepare us for the reproductive roles of adults, but our minds are still developing, and our ability to make sound decisions doesn't necessarily come with this change. Some teens fear this; they don't understand what's happening to their body. I didn't really experience a huge bodily transformation. My breast and butt were always small.

I was a social teen, always into something but not everyone develops the social personality. For some, this is okay, but for others, the lack of social skills and/or a few good friends can be a huge stunt in development. Many ignore or tease these kids. Others write them off by assuming, "It's just them" or "It is a phase they will grow out of." One must consider what may be a factor in their lack of socialization. Now, don't get me wrong, everyone doesn't want to have a group of friends, but everyone needs someone to talk to, especially as a teen.

Though everyone would love to have an ideal relationship with their parents, this isn't always the case. Your relationship with your parents will have highs and lows, and though our parents are supposed to encourage us as children, this doesn't always happen. Parents didn't get a rule book on how to parent, and most parents teach from their experiences. Parents and children try to do their best to satisfy the perceived needs of the other, which can result in the development of a mask. One of the reasons for this is that past behavior can cause so much pain that you try to hide the person that your family tried to make you out to be. I don't think that parents realize the effect that they have on their kids, nor are they conscious of the long-term implications for the child's future growth and development.

I'm speaking as a parent and knowing the harm that I've caused my kids and the pain my parents caused me. It's funny because every time I get mad at my kids and start yelling, I later regret some of the things I say, and I beat myself up, wishing that I would've handled things differently. But, we all know, once you say it, there are no take backs. You can ask for forgiveness, try to convince them you didn't mean it and you're sorry. If they're young, they will forgive you, and everything will be normal; if they're teenagers, they will begin to dislike things about you. Nobody is perfect; mistakes are made daily, so don't sweep it under the rug. Always follow up with your children and see how they're processing what happened.

My mom was verbally and physically abusive when she was mad or drunk. I grew up and imitated some of that same behavior in my dealings with my loved ones. I would use my words to hurt my child or someone else I loved because I had been hurt with words over and over again. I didn't realize the damage I had done until my son had become a teenager. We were talking about the past, and he expressed how he didn't like it when I told him he was going to be like his father. To him, I was saying he was going to be a failure. Of course, that wasn't my intention at the time. I don't look at his dad as a failure; I don't even know why I used that to get him to want to do right. I respect his father, but he sees him differently than I see him.

Just think about how many times you've said some mean things to your child in hopes of change in their behavior. Why? It's something that's programmed in our minds in the black community, we are quick to say what we not gonna do, what we taking from them, all these empty threats and for what? Because that doesn't make them change; it might get them to start doing it. The thing with that is now you've pierced your child with all these negative images. I'm sure I said it out of frustration, but it wasn't for him to think I was calling him a failure. It broke my heart to know that I caused my son to feel like this. I immediately apologized to him and showed him how much I believed in him. I know he's destined for greatness. The problem with that is, I had already planted that seed in his head, regardless of how long ago I said it–this was something he had been living with for a long time, and I didn't know it. Just thinking about it makes me sad all over again because I know that I've said so many hurtful things to him without realizing what I was saying.

Speaking when angry, unhappy, or frustrated serves no valuable purpose. I know there should have been limits when it came to my son, but because there were no limits with my parents when dealing with me, I had no limits either. It was learned behavior. From the day that I found out I was pregnant with him, I loved him and knew he was chosen by God to be my son. As a matter of fact, I knew I was having a son ever since I was a little girl. When I was younger, I had one of those real dolls that had real private parts, and my doll was a boy. Come to think of it, I only had two dolls my whole life, that boy baby and a cabbage patch doll when I was five years old. Dolls were never my thing though. I preferred to hang outside playing basketball, dodgeball, kickball, hide go seek, four square, hide go get it, handball and a bunch of other childhood games. Though many people have a negative perception of the projects, some of them warranted; overall though, growing up in the projects was a lot of fun because we were all family. Even though I had some personal issues to deal with, I really appreciate everything about where I grew up and who I grew up with. I love my Valencia Garden Family. Growing up in the projects had their pros and cons. I personally felt it had more pros than cons for me, even though I've been living with a mask since I was a child. In the projects, it didn't matter what mask I had on; Monique was always accepted.

Being a social teen can be good because it allows you to experience so much during your high school years. However, at the same time, it can be stressful trying to keep up with the popularity, and that can cause you to put on a mask because now you have to maintain this image of what everyone thinks of you. When you have the need to be accepted by others, you can easily lose yourself.

The desire to be accepted becomes more important than the desire to be yourself. Losing yourself can cause insecurities within, and that can be a hard wall to breakthrough. When you're used to putting the mask on during your teenage years, knowing the real you is slim to none. You might ask, why do I say that? I will tell you, the reason is, you're being pulled in so many different directions when you're a teenager, so if you don't know who you are, you fall into a deeper hole. Though this can be scary, we must power through if we want to do the work necessary to rediscover our authentic selves. Go through the process, and by the time you are done with this book; you should be one step closer to actualizing your purpose. This book is all about developing the Never Personal, Always Purpose mindset and walking in the Power of Purpose.

Having siblings or multiple children can also be the cause of the mask coming on. I have two sisters, one older and one younger; I also have an older brother, and when we were growing up, I was the trouble child. I was the one that they picked on. I was the one that had it harder because of the trouble my older siblings would get in. My parents would be mad at them and sometimes, this would trickle down to them being frustrated with me. My parents were so busy paying attention to what my older sister was doing that they missed everything happening with me. I can't believe that so many things happened to me as a kid, and I had done so many things that nobody really knew about. They were too distracted by their own lives. It was so bad that I had to put on a mask with my siblings and parents. I had to make them think I was the perfect little girl. I needed them to think that I wasn't doing the things I was doing: dealing drugs, humping girls and boys, stealing their money, and so much more that's a shadow in my mind.

My mask consisted of me being fast like my sister and then being a boy like my brother. The funny thing is, nobody knew the fast girl except the person that I was fast with. I had everyone fooled with my mask. I never revealed my mask; it was something that I had to live with forever, and it had a huge effect on me as I got older. Pay attention to your children! Don't think it's funny when they show you grownup behavior. You have to know that children pay more attention than we want to believe; think back to all the things you knew about your parents without them telling you. Don't let your child or yourself be a victim to the mask another day. My mask was developed to help me, and now I'm convinced that it caused me more harm than good. I wish I were strong enough to face my truth in each moment that the mask came on. This could have prevented me from living with a cloud over me most of my life. It's funny because even though I felt that I was strong, confident and secure in who I was, the truth is I lived most of my life in fear. Not because I was scared of someone knowing the person under the mask, but because I didn't know the person under the mask.

Writing this book is my release, being able to tell my truth isn't easy, but I know revealing my truth will help everyone reading it. This book is opening my eyes more and more to the power of purpose. Siblings have a huge impact on the person that we become regardless of their age differences; my older sister is older by four years, and I'm eight years older than my younger sister. The impact that we had on each other's lives was huge. We were close growing up because our mom always kept us together, yet we lived totally different lives. Of all my parents' kids, I'm the only one that sold drugs, went to jail, and married into a same-sex relationship. Sometimes, I wonder if these things were because of my experiences inside or outside of my home?

Though I think about it often, I believe this is something I will never know. I can only assume that it was a culmination of all my experiences. I was a beast in the streets. I would be rude and dis-respectful to my clients. Though there were times when I was 'Nice,' for the most part, I was mean—it was part of my image. It was a manifestation of the mask. Living a street life was hard and really took a toll on me because I had to make sure I kept up with the hardest men on the block. Now don't get me wrong; they were nice to me, and we were all like family. Family had nothing to do with making money, though, and it was everyone for themselves un-less you were linked up with your boyfriend/girlfriend. If that was the case, they were getting money together. Selling drugs was a man's hustle, but there were plenty of girls who sold drugs with or without their boyfriends. We were all out there like one big crew; thousands came flowing through our projects every day. This is a part of my past. I am not proud of what I had done. I was mean and violent, but I did what I believed I had to do to survive at that time of my life; I was being who I had to be at that moment. Had it not been for those experiences, I would not be the woman I am to-day.

I'm so glad that I was able to take the mask I wore off when I was done selling drugs. I knew how to switch masks and be who I needed to be in every situation I was in. Looking back, it amazes me how my personalities of myself were normal to my par-ents because looking back; it seems off to me. It wasn't until I was in my early 30s that I started to remove one mask at a time. The first mask to go was the mask of the drug dealer, and I'm glad it happened. Though my siblings knew about this mask, my parents didn't until I got arrested for selling drugs at age 16. At that point, I had been selling drugs for six years. My dad was so disappointed in me. He couldn't believe it, which was a shock to me. How could he not know when he was the one that taught me the game? He was the one that told me what to do and what not to do. He was spending a lot of time talking at me instead of talking with me. See, the problem was that in his mind, he was just telling me about his business, and I turned it into my own business.

When I would get around them, I had to be their sweet daughter who played basketball and worked a typical teenager's job. I wore a mask at work also. I had a job at KFC. I was a very cheerful cashier, pleasing the customers and always giving them 100% customer service. I was so good that in six months, I was promoted to be Assistant Manager. This was no surprise to the family, especially since I had grown up working inside KFC as a little girl with my uncle and aunt, who were both managers at different KFCs. I had all of these personalities to juggle, but I knew how to be who I needed to be at that moment. It was easy for me to put on these different masks throughout the day because I started putting my mask on as a kid. It became my normal.

The girl that played basketball was fun, wild and supportive of her team. She was the popular girl in the school, had a variety of friends, didn't hang with the same crowd every day because she was a free spirit. She didn't care about what anyone thought about her different personas because her mask had nothing to do with them. She was okay with being different. Now, you might say, "if you are so different, why wear the mask"? The reason for the mask was that it provided a feeling of safety in being whoever she wanted or needed to be at that moment. It's also important to acknowledge that she never realized how many masks she wore. The reason I'm talking about myself in the third person, saying "she" and not "I" is because each of the masks I put on represented another personality in me. The funny thing is that, as I'm writing this, I have a better understanding of the many masks that I put on and the reasons for each mask.

What I realized is that because nobody paid attention to any of the warning signs I manifested in my youth, my behavior at the time was normal to everyone. When I was 19 years old, I had my son. I was now a mommy. I really enjoyed being a mother. When I was in mommy mode, nothing else mattered. I would stop doing everything when I was in mommy mode. There was no selling drugs and no hanging out. My son was the most important thing to me. I didn't let him spend the night at anybody's house when he was a baby. Once he turned one, that all changed. I got more involved with hanging out all around the city and not just my block. Along with that, I had enrolled my son in daycare, and since I didn't have a real job, I spent my time on the streets hustling while he was at daycare, and on weekends, he would go with his grandparents. So I took off the mommy mask more than it was on when my son was younger. I wish I could have done things differently with my son; I question myself all the time.

Why did I love being in the streets? Why couldn't I work a regular job and then go home to my son? Where did the disconnect come in between me and my son? Writing these questions made things clear. Had I chosen to remove the drug dealing mask when I had my son, things would have been different for both of us. Then again, had I not made those choices, I might not be in the position I am today; to tell my story of how I stepped into my purpose. The mask of the street girl was on most of the time. I graduated from high school but dropped out of college because I got pregnant with my son. Once I re-enrolled, the classes seemed less interesting to me.

Then there was the baby mama mask. I was the perfect girlfriend. I was everything that my son's father needed me to be. I made sure he had all that he needed. He had anger issues when things went wrong on the block for him, so I would do all that I could to keep him calm. That was a hard task, especially since we were both hustling on the same block. When he would lose something or stash his drugs somewhere, and someone would take it, that was like World War 2 for me. Even though he wasn't mad at me; I was the one that was taking the heat. I remember once someone took his shoes out of our car. He was so mad. I went to get him another pair of shoes, and though it didn't make it better at that time, things went back to normal after a few hours. I didn't realize how much he was draining me, but it was a lot. His mood could change in the blink of an eye, so I found myself constantly on eggshells to protect his feelings and his happiness.

This went on for about three years until he admitted to me that he'd cheated on me. I was crushed. I couldn't believe that after all that I had done for him, all that I was doing for him, he found time to cheat on me. He had gone to jail more than once, and I was there every weekend with bells on. Whenever he needed something, it was always on me: "Me" who made sure he never missed commissary. "Me." Now, I can't say that none of that mattered to him because I am sure that it did. The cheating happened while I was pregnant, and that was something that I couldn't forgive. It didn't matter to me that it was one time or what excuse he had; what mattered was the fact that he'd cheated. He didn't love, respect, or value me nor our relationship the way that I did. He wasn't in love with the idea of us being the perfect family. He would say that he was, but his actions didn't line up with what he was saying.

I'm an action person. I need to see action; I can care less about words as they can have too many empty promises. I learned that making excuses for staying only makes the pain worse and doesn't allow the heart to heal. I tried to stay with my son's father because I loved the idea of having my family more than I loved myself. I thought I could settle and forgive, but that wasn't possible because my heart was broken. So, instead of being the committed girlfriend that I was, I was the cheating baby mama until enough was enough. Because of the heartbreak I experienced with him, I put on a new mask. He crushed my dreams of having a family, and now I had a heart of steel. The girl that once trusted and felt that it was nasty to be with two people now believed that nobody could only be with one person. Just because someone breaks your heart or you break someone's heart doesn't mean that you will have this same behavior in your next relationship.

I began to carry every relationship the same, and doing that wasn't fair to me or the person I was with. When a relationship doesn't go right, don't play the blame game. Learn something valuable from the relationship, take that time to know what you like and don't like in a person. When you find that special someone that you believe is the one, don't feel like you have to do things differently and be someone that you're not. I had seen that forever with my parents; they were together until they went home with the Lord. It was rare to see both parents in the home in the projects, but we were that rare family. I quickly learned that just because I was raised like that and understood what it takes to be in a committed relationship doesn't mean that everyone else does.

When I broke up with my son's father, I realized that it did something to me mentally. The betrayal was so devastating that I allowed his behavior to change the way that I felt about relationships. I took his behavior personally- "he must not love me," "I'm not good enough for him," but it may not have been that at all. He was a product of his environment, just as I was. He was living the lifestyle he had seen growing up, and I was trying to do the same. I know this now, but I didn't understand it then. So, now my guard has gone up when it comes to men.

I have a great relationship now with my son's father now. We were better off as co-parents. It's hard to co-parent once you've had the family, and I think this is why many stay in unhealthy relationships, making it about the kids, years or time spent. What matters the most is how a person treats you and having the security to believe in that person to love, honor, protect, comfort, respect, and support you through your high and low times. Settling should never be an option; it will always hurt in the long run, and being with someone for any other reason than being attracted to them physically or mentally is the wrong reason. You either fall in love with their look or their mind; if it's their money, fame or your lack of security, those are the wrong reasons.

I had this guy named MD who'd been trying to talk to me for months, and I kept turning him down. I finally gave in, and we went on a date to Pier 39, which was so much fun. We continued to date for a couple of years. So now the girlfriend mask was back on. He liked that I was hood smart, and I liked that he was hood. After a couple of years, things started to get different. He started staying out late or not coming home at all. Of course, he always had an excuse and was able to use the hustle because in the streets you could be out all-night hustling. The only reason I would believe that story is because I've also stayed out all night hustling on the block. We all know that what's in the dark comes to the light. I found out that he was cheating on me. I had enough; I wasn't about to settle for that. I didn't settle with my son's father, and I wasn't about to start now. I immediately kicked him out of my house and because of that, a new mask emerged; the mask of the cheater. This mask had come on before, but I didn't think anything of it because I was cheating with my son's father, so in my eyes that wasn't cheating because I loved him; this is how dysfunctional my thinking was.

The mask of the cheater was easier to adapt to than I thought it would be. Let me give you some context. When I was younger, I had boyfriends that nobody knew about. I did things with boys that nobody knows, except for them and me. One day, I was thinking about my life and had a very disturbing revelation. When I was younger, I was violated by some of the adult males in my life. This is where the fast-little girl mask came from. Though only a few people knew of her, I am still baffled that no one put forth the effort to find out where she came from. It pains me that I cannot have these conversations with my parents. I can't tell them how I was violated as a young girl, how the people they trusted in our house or trusted me to get in the car with had violated their baby girl. I lived with this secret for my whole life. I didn't have these type of thoughts until I had to help some of my students work through their emotions of being violated. When you bury past trauma, it will always resurface. If this has sparked some emotions for you that you've been keeping inside, let it out, find that special someone you trust and release the pain. You might be thinking it's in the past and that's where you want it to stay, but it's never going to truly be in the past until you release it.

Writing this has opened a lot of old wounds for me. I'm understanding more and more where my mask first came from. Mone' had to come out because Monique needed to be protected. At least, that is what she thought. So, instead of being committed to one guy, Mone' chose to be committed to me and do what she felt was right for me so that I wouldn't continue to feel betrayed or lied to. So, now I was the girl with multiple boyfriends. I wasn't sleeping with them all, but I would keep a few dudes on reserve if the one I was really into started acting up. I had friends in different cities. It didn't matter how many friends I had, as when I was with each one, he felt that he was the only one. I began to play the same game that was played on me by the boys I was with previously. I call them boys because, in my eyes, that's how they were acting, like little boys, immature, irresponsible, and out for themselves. See, a grown man knew how to take care of his woman, family and home. My daddy was my example of a real man.

I look back at this girl, and I feel sorry for her. All those years, I didn't realize that I was wearing a mask. I thought that I had it all together when the reality is, I was broken inside and, in turn, I was breaking everyone that was trying to love me because of how bad I had been hurt. I thought I was in love, but I never had a chance to release that pain because of the heartbreak paired with the violation I experienced as a child. I'm very blessed to be able to release this pain through writing. My truth is my truth, and today the mask comes off. I will not be held a prisoner in my mind any longer for any of the things that happened to me, whether in my control or not. I wore the mask of a cheater and heartbreaker for many years. I couldn't bring myself to trust any man, no matter how good he was to me. I also kept all men away from my son. I wasn't looking for a stepfather for him because my son had a daddy.

As far as I was concerned, all a guy could do for me was to fill my sexual needs. I had my own money, car and house. I didn't care to hear all those sweet nothings; I love you, you're so pretty, you're my only one or none of that. In my mind, it was all lies and them just telling me what they thought I wanted to hear. I look back and realize that some really loved me, but they couldn't love me the way I deserved to be loved because I didn't know how to love myself. Growing up and living the street life isn't as easy as it seemed to be for me back then. It really caused a lot of socio-emotional issues, and the worst part about that is these issues aren't being addressed in the hood. I think this is why so many people from the hood end up in jail or dead because of the lack of attention to the mental and emotional toll the environment has on its community members.

Who's challenging their parents about being a good/bad parent when you're young? Nobody and this is why so many issues never get addressed. I've watched many dysfunctional families go through life without any regard to why things were the way they were. It's important for parents to get the help they need to be good parents and not reflect all the things that they didn't like onto their child. It's even more important for parents to pay attention to the behavior of their child when around them and when around others. Parents have a busy life, which can cause a lot of things to be overlooked when it comes to raising kids. When your kid(s) are overlooked, it can be a problem now or when they become adults. It's in the best interest of everyone if matters are addressed as they arise and not swept under the rug.

Now, let's fast forward to the mask of the lesbian. This mask felt more real, free, and like me. While serving five years in federal prison, I discovered that I really liked women, so I started to talk to different women in prison. I was having a good time having multiple girls wanting me. I got comfortable with this mask. I told my family that I was with women, and this was going to be my lifestyle moving forward. The hard part was telling my son. So even though the mask came off with everyone else, the mask stayed on with him. I was ashamed of what he might think of me and how he would receive me as his mom. I waited until I came home from prison to tell him, and it was the worst ever. He was 11 years old, and he didn't take it so well. He didn't understand why I didn't like a man. He wondered why I couldn't just be like everybody else? Why couldn't I be normal? These were some of the things he said to me. My heart broke at first as he didn't want to kiss me or drink from the same cup as me, as he did before. I didn't know how to handle that at first, and we began seeing a therapist.

Unfortunately, this didn't work out too well because, during our sessions, she disclosed things that I wasn't comfortable with him knowing at the time. As his mother, it was my job to work through this with him. I had to explain to him that this was my normal and what my sexual preference is doesn't change the way that I love him or me being his mom. It took a while but eventually, he was okay with it. I never thought my son had any issues with other kids about me being in a same-sex relationship. He never had any phone calls home, fights, or any alarms that would have made me think this. One day, we were talking about him being in school, and he told me that he had to defend me a lot, and he had many issues at school because of my sexual preference. I was sad when he told me this because I was too busy thinking everything was normal. But how could it be when being in a same-sex relationship isn't normal? Parents, don't assume that everything is okay just because nobody is calling home. Be sure to ask your child questions about who, what, where, when and why. Don't just settle for okay, good, nothing, or alright. If you want your child and yourself to be able to work through things, you have to start now.

I never introduced my son to any of my ex-girlfriends as my girlfriend. With my wife, it was different. I introduced my son to her, and he was okay with it. Don't get me wrong; I have introduced my son to other girls that I was sleeping with, but it was as my friend and not my girlfriend. He was even okay with us moving in together as a family, and I was so relieved. It was so great and perfect for me because what I had once viewed as a mask was now revealing itself to be a true manifestation of who I am. See, for you to really know the person behind the mask, you have to know why the mask came on and who it comes on for. Once these things become clear to you, then you can start the steps needed to remove the mask and see the person in the mirror. Some people think they can just remove the mask whenever they want, and that is true, to a certain degree. Just as I was able to remove the mask whenever I wanted, with every removal came another mask, and I would imagine this is the same for most of you. It's very important for you to be honest with yourself. Break the wall that you have up and really do some reflecting on the who, where, when, why, or how's of your life. Just like you want to know these things for everyone in your life.

Answering these questions for yourself will give you a better understanding of how to proceed. This is not going to be easy; it can be a very challenging and very emotional experience. This emotional rollercoaster is going to test your courage, faith, strength and determination, even for those of us who believe ourselves to be riding a wave of emotion already. Remember, even though you look at yourself in the mirror every day, it's possible not to know the person you stare at day after day. I hope that once you're done reading this book, you will have a clearer understanding of who you see and how to become the person you want to be, the person you truly are, and all that is possible with the Power Of Purpose.

I'm shocked by all the pain I've endured as a child, especially because nobody was there to protect me. I didn't know that riding on my uncle's lap as a kid was violating me. I didn't know to speak up and tell my mom or dad that I felt something, and it didn't feel normal. I know that my mom and dad would have protected me. I know they would've done something to my uncles, but I didn't know to ask my parents about what was happening because this was all normal for me as a kid. Why would they think that my uncles were being inappropriate with their innocent niece? They thought nothing of it and at the time, neither did I. The messed-up part is, I feel these inappropriate actions go deeper than just this, but I have nobody that can give me answers. I don't even know if they felt like everything was innocent, but the way my spirit feels about it lets me know it was wrong. This has traumatized me to the point that I don't like to see little girls sitting on a man's lap. I don't care who the man is: her dad, grandpa, brother, or uncle. In my opinion, little girls don't need to sit in-between a man's leg. I think back to all those times I would drive on my uncle's lap as a little girl, and it makes me sick to my stomach. Just think about that small space, I was sitting my ass right on his private area. My heart breaks thinking about it. I don't fault my parents because they didn't know. Nothing on the surface was questionable. However, I've been living with these questions my whole life and didn't know it until now. I'm grateful that God gave me the courage to write this book and share my story, and I pray that my story helps you to tell your story.

See, now I can look back and see that the things that were done to me weren't personal. They had issues as men. They lacked something. They were broken and hurt. Did someone hurt them when they were kids? Is this why they hurt me? I will never really know the answer to these questions and, in some ways, the answers are irrelevant because it was their behavior, for better and for worse, that led me on the path that has brought me to this point in my life. Telling my story to help women or men all around the world, who may be struggling with removing the masks that they've had to live with for most of their life. The purpose behind the pain is the strength that it's given me.

I'm a very strong woman today. My strength comes from my pain, and the strength to remove the mask and love the person in the mirror comes from the Power of Purpose. I went through some serious issues growing up, and I'm grateful that God blessed me to overcome it all and find purpose through the storm. When people hurt you, it's easy to make it personal and make it about you. When it's not about you, the problem is within them, and they don't have the courage to face it. They put it off on other people, hurting them and causing them pain, just like what was done to me. Let's take back our power, let's take ownership for the person we're today, not because of our past but because this is the person from those experiences. You can live with the mask forever, or you can release the mask now and begin to embrace the person you see. Living with the mask continues to give each of those reasons for the mask the power over you. It's time to take back your power and let the Power Of Purpose be in control.

Poem:

When I was in the womb, I was free, pure and innocent

The baby me is unsure of who, what, where, when, why and how

I'm sure I would always stare into the clouds

Being guided by the Spirit and not the loud sounds

With growth came the people that tricked me like a clown

Causing the mask to come on and never hit the ground

I was protected by my other half

I felt it all, I could not laugh

My pain is part of my past

I will no longer wear a mask

By: Monique Turner

Chapter 2:
Understanding Who You Are

When I first began to understand a little bit about myself, I was in prison; I was alone, I had lost both my parents and left my son and family behind. Even though I was on a huge case with over 30 codefendants, I had to go to federal prison all alone. Of course, there were lots of other women in prison with me, but none that I knew personally. When I was first indicted, I was with one of my girl codefendants (Unicorn) until I went home on bail; of course, this is before I was sentenced. I was happy that I was able to see her, and she gave me some hygiene and food to hold me over until I could shop. I really appreciated her then and now. We went from being codefendants of a federal case with a no-contact order to women with a passion for business and a purpose that involves helping others. I was blessed to be able to go home and get things in order before I had to serve my five years.

The person that I had been on the streets my whole life didn't matter in prison. In prison, I had to be the prison girl; this girl didn't have a mask because this was someone that I had to learn how to adapt to, this was a new experience that could go good or bad. I'm really blessed that my prison experience was great; I got to meet some cool women that I'm still in contact with today. We were like a big happy family. We cooked, played sports, watched TV, washed clothes, worked, slept, and cried together. I had done more with these ladies that were strangers to me than I did with the people that I'd grown up with my whole life.

Prison opened me up, and I could be to myself if I wanted. When I was on the streets, I was always with Cousin, Qui, or other girls from my hood. Being yourself in prison can be a long miserable sentence, as all you have in prison is the girls, TV, commissary, phone calls and visits every weekend. The unfortunate part is some people don't have any of these things, but I was blessed to have them all. I was blessed to have my little sister, who did a lot being only 18. She took really good care of me and my son. My cousin/sister also was my lifesaver, and she took care of me and my son. She never missed a beep, she answered every call, made every visit and let my son live with her when he wanted to leave his granny's house.

I'm forever grateful for Krystal and my siblings. My little brother (Mo-Cat) and his wife (Nona) would always send me money and come see me. Everyone took turns seeing me, making sure I had visits every weekend and enough money to shop. My older brother and sister also took good care of me, and they would visit when they could. My son's father was also there for me as I had been there for him when he was incarcerated. The one that shocked me the most was Jelly. I was now with women, and he still made sure to always send me money, cards and even came to visit. I'm really blessed that I had so much support. I'm blessed how they all accepted the person that Monique became in prison.

I started having same-sex relations quickly, which I let everyone know as they came to visit me. The only person I didn't let know while I was in prison is my son who I stated in Chapter one. Even though my look had changed from hair done with flat irons to hair being braided, he didn't see anything wrong with that. All he cared about was seeing his mother, and since I started my same-sex relations just about as soon as I got there, I had four years to live this lifestyle and really know if it was what I wanted once I returned home. Especially since I had a boyfriend (Jelly) before I went to prison and had never been with a woman before. The funny thing about that is although I'd never been with another woman, I was with another girl when I was a kid. I would play house with some of my girl cousins and friends, and we would hump each other. Where did that behavior come from? I have no idea; it's only something I can look back on now and know that somehow, all that we encountered since birth has something to do with our purpose in life, and in order to understand that purpose, you have to tap into everything about you, the good, the bad, the buried deep and the surface.

Therefore, I'm going through my life piece by piece, because without each piece, I wouldn't be able to discover the real me. You need to be willing to do the same thing. I need you to be willing to accept all the challenges that come with understanding who you are. Some people will think that because you're living a good life, big house, husband/wife, family, a career job, boat, or CEO of your own business that you know who you are. That's not always true. Your finances don't dictate who you are; it just shows that you have made a good living for yourself, and you know how to save or invest your money. It could even be that you come from money and don't have a clue about being independent. That has nothing to do with your spirit, your soul, tapping into your spirit plays a big role in who you are.

Facing the ugly truth can be terrifying for many, especially if you don't know how to deal with your emotions. Some people are so emotional that they start crying behind TV programs, kids crying, or their friends feeling sad. It could be very difficult for a person like this. It's also very difficult to face these things when you're weak within. The only way to be strengthened from within is to release everything, all those private thoughts, the pretty and the ugly. You can't hold back; you must pray on it, ask God to give you strength through your process of revealing and healing. This will be the worst emotional rollercoaster ride that you get on, but once you get off, it would have been the best ride of your life because all that pain, anger, trauma and frustration that you once endured can now be behind you. This is easier said than done, so let's stay on track before I get ahead of myself.

Okay, now that I'm confident in being Monique, the girl in a same-sex relationship, I feel that I can't be with men anymore. My mind was letting me know that when I get home, I'm going to be with women. I let everybody know this, even the guy I was with before I went to jail. He was so good to me; we had only been together for fun, and I knew I was going to prison, and so did he. He kept telling me that he was going to hold me down while I was gone. I didn't believe him, but he did. Of course, he fell off from time to time, but I didn't care as I was living my life in here, and I knew he had to continue to live his life out there. He questioned me about a few of my friends, asking me if I was with them when I was on the streets, and I told him time and time again that my first adult relations with a woman started in prison. He was like my best friend, and the fun we had was real. Being honest about my life came easy, and even though I wore multiple masks, I was always honest about me.

Everyone was okay with it; they even felt that they'd known I would be like this, although I'm not sure how they knew that. Maybe because I was what they used to call a "tomboy," which was the girl that did boy things and hung out with boys all the time and yes, that was me. This made it easy for most people to accept, I guess. Then, there were a few friends that were uncomfortable at times. I was okay with that because this was my lifestyle, not their's. The blessing is they never switched up; they were worried about what people would think if they saw us together, not knowing if they were my friend or my girlfriend. Now, this shouldn't matter, but it does when you're the type of person that cares about what people think. Caring about what people think of you will stop you from doing what you really want to do. Instead of doing what you want, you hold back, caring more about their perception of you.

This can really be a big problem when you're trying to step into your purpose. You can't step into your purpose, living in fear of what people might think of you. I'm so glad coming out was easy for me because I felt that my family would accept me, I have a couple of uncles that were in same-sex relationships, and my family loved them, so I knew that they would continue loving me. Once my prison sentence was over, I was stepping into my authentic self, one step at a time. I was fighting the battle within myself, do I continue to be the street girl that everybody knew, or was I supposed to be different because I was coming home to be with a woman and not a man? Now it was even more interesting because even though I'm a girl, I acted more like a boy.

This is what selling drugs and hustling will do to you. The girls I hung with even acted like boys but had boyfriends. So, now I was able to have that boy image, it was so weird and normal at the same time, if that makes sense. I was getting familiar with Monique being back on the streets because when you're in prison, that's another world that could never compare to life on the streets. The good thing that came out of prison for me is that I was able to release the person that I never knew was inside of me. I was able to explore another side of myself. I've always had these opportunities on the streets, but for whatever reason, it never happened besides when I was a kid.

Everything is aligned with God's purpose for our life, and some of us realize this young, old or never. My life didn't begin to make sense until I received God as the Father, the head of my life. When I came home from prison, life was real. I had a son who was now 11, and I needed to be responsible for him, support him, love him, and raise him. He lived with his granny most of the time I was in prison, and before that, she would always watch him whenever I needed a babysitter or whenever he wanted to come over. Granny was his everything and still is today; she's my son's father's grandmother. She was a very special lady, and I love her so much for accepting me and loving me as if I was her own. I even called her Granny. She passed away a few months after I came home from prison.

Before I went to prison, I had it all together. I had the money, cars, clothes, man, house and street credibility. I thought I was living the good life; it was the good life alright; it was the life of life lessons. When I came home, I had to start over. I needed all new clothes since my style had changed, but I was blessed to still have my apartment. My little sister moved in with me before I had to go to prison, so I wouldn't lose my apartment. This was a blessing because even though I had nothing, meaning material items, I had a roof over our heads. I tried to keep life as normal as I could for my son. It took for my son to express that he would rather spend time with me instead of having material items. That's when I had to rethink my whole life, and giving up the streets is what was first on the list. I didn't come home doing the right thing, as even though I had found what my sexual preference was, I still didn't know what my purpose was. I was caught up in the street me, getting money the best way I knew how and by any means necessary. I was battling with doing the right thing and doing what I was used to.

See, when you're fighting the battle of trying to get rid of your old habits and create new ones, the enemy is always hard at work. The enemy doesn't want you to step into the person God created you to be, and this was the case for me. I was on the fence of doing good, trying to work and support my son, but the enemy wanted to keep me in the gutter. God quickly interrupted that when he put me back in the half way house for something so silly, something that had nothing to do with me. I was in the wrong place at the wrong time. I know now it was all about the lesson for me; it was all about God showing me who he was and how my life was going in the wrong direction. I knew that if I continued doing it my way, I was headed to self-destruction real fast. My path had to change quickly. Even though I was trying to do right, I was still hanging around the same people that were doing wrong and in the same environment where drugs were being sold. I had to switch it up. I couldn't continue this path, or I could end up back in prison.

I called an old friend of mine, "E," and she told me about this church that she goes to that was near my house. I decided to go; the word was powerful, that didn't bring change, that brought the word, the change began to happen when things started to happen, and it was clear to me that it was God. I would always watch TD. Jakes and Joyce Myers on TV when I was in prison, and one of my good friends helped me during my time of grieving. I would lose my mind every year during my daddy's birthday. I was blessed that my friend came into my room to see if I was okay. She introduced God into my life, and I started to pray for my roommate. She hadn't talked to her daughter in years, and that was my prayer to God for her to speak with her daughter. A few months went by and then just like that, she came into my room so happy; she had finally spoken with her daughter.

I knew this was God. This was the first time I'd seen him answer one of my prayers. Even though I had seen this happen, I still felt like I didn't have faith in him; I didn't believe in him. Why would I? He took both my mom and dad. I was angry with him for this. How could there be a God that sends people through so much pain, that takes the only parents you have? I had nobody to help me when things got tough. This was my mindset; thinking like this was bad for me. It caused me to grieve wrong and feel like I was all alone when, in reality, God had been comforting me in a way that no other living soul could. I didn't understand this back then. I understand it now because of being aware of who I am.

Knowing who I am came with a price to pay. Just as I let go of a lot of old habits, I had to let go of some longtime friends and family. Everybody isn't a part of the process you will have to go through in order to grow. You must be willing to do that on your own, and you must be okay with being alone. I was thankful that prison taught me that even though I was cool with everybody and always had a girlfriend, I was moody and needed time to myself. I'd never been the reader type, but I started to read while I was in prison, and this would occupy hours of my time throughout the day. I did most of my reading in my room or outside. I find peace listening to the sounds of the wind and the ocean. You must find your place of peace, a place that you can go to physically or in your mind. See, when I can't reach the ocean, putting the window down or sitting outside will do. I find peace in my bedroom, enjoying my own private thoughts.

The biggest battle we all face daily is the battle in our mind. See, life sent me through opposition after opposition. If I hadn't begun to reflect on my past life, seeing how every part of my life was a lesson for the purpose ahead, I don't know if I would have ever found peace, because instead of seeing the purpose, I was taking everything personally. Once I finally settled down and got married, the search for love was over, and the need to be these different people was finally over. With my wife, I was able to be Monique. Now, you might be saying you've always been Monique. Well, I've always needed a mask on, but now the mask was completely off, and the new beginning had just begun. I knew the Monique whose sexual preference was women, but I didn't know the wife Monique, the faithful Monique, the Monique that was putting her wife and kids' needs before hers. I knew this Monique when I was 18, with my son's father. That was over 20 years ago, and multiple masks had developed since then.

The good thing for me is, she was dealing with some of the same issues as me, so we had some masks that we had to learn how to remove together. I had never been faithful to a woman. I'd cheated on all my previous girlfriends, not because they cheated on me or did anything wrong. I was ruined. I know that I loved everyone that I had a relationship with, but I wasn't in love with them, and that's a huge difference. I didn't believe in being in love or being faithful to anybody, and my heart was on reserve until I met my wife. This was all I knew, and this was all a part of the journey of me getting to know Monique. My wife and I fell in love at first sight. We married in six months and have been together for 10 years now. In the beginning, I was a wreck emotionally when we got together. I was struggling with all the baggage from before: the loss of my parents, being cheated on, going to prison, leaving my son, being the cheater, financial insecurities, and so much more.

I didn't realize how much of a wreck I was until I found my soulmate, the person that I wanted to make happy and give the world to. She had always given me her all and supported me emotionally and financially without ever throwing it in my face, and that still wasn't good enough to give me peace of mind. Every time I was frustrated with myself because what I was trying to do wasn't working with the hustle or I was looking for a job; I would take it out on her, causing us to argue for no reason. I was unhappy within, and this was making my wife unhappy with me, which was slowly taking its toll on our marriage. Finally, after about three years, a light bulb went off in my head, and I started to see that I was more of the problem instead of the solution. If I wanted my marriage to last, I needed to do some reevaluating of myself and fast. I needed to stop blaming her for my own insecurities and trust issues. Because I didn't trust anybody for all those years, it made it hard for me to trust her. I would follow her sometimes to make sure she was going where she said she was going, and that was bad.

Let me rewind. When my wife and I first got together, we were both with other people, even though we ended our previous relationships, that didn't happen until after six months of dating. You know what they say, "how you get them is how you lose them." This played in my head for years, but after playing stalker for a few months and seeing that she was always telling me the truth, I started to really trust her. I was insecure and afraid of being cheated on because I was vulnerable, and so I did some crazy things. Fear will eat at you; fear will make you play a bunch of tricks in your head for nothing; living in fear will cause you to see things from the wrong lens. I was making things harder than they needed to be for my wife and me. I realized that I'd found someone that I loved, and I didn't want to continue to hurt her or me. I see the issues, and now I need to do something about it to set a solid foundation for our kids to grow up in, especially since our household is abnormal to society.

What's normal to you can be abnormal to others and vice versa. You can't live your life worried about pleasing other people. Trying to please those around you or those you love can cause you to lose your true self, instead of knowing your true self. The only person you will know is the person that you've tried to be for your loved ones. Just think about it. If I would have never got the courage to tell my son that I was in a same-sex relationship, then I wouldn't be free now. I would have continued living the life that was normal for him and not myself. Therefore, it's important to tap into your authentic self, know your likes, dislikes, wants, desires, triggers, happiness, peace, romance, and what you look for in a relationship and why. This is a key factor for you to know who you are, and reliving the past is the only thing that brought me out of those bad habits that I couldn't let go. Those habits were my normal.

I didn't see anything wrong with the way that I treated the people I was in a relationship with: my friends, kids, family and all connected to me. I was known for being sweet my whole life, but I was also known for being a badass kid, sassy mouth, talk too much, tomboy, pre-teen hustler, athlete, leader, and the adult me was a hustler, mother, cool, fun, rude, leader, spiritual, therapist, pastor, and loving. These are a few things that come to mind that I can remember being called when I was coming up, and those words defined me because I let them. I didn't stand against who they thought I was; I allowed myself to believe that I was the person that everyone called me instead of trying to really know who I was. Because of that, most of my life, I have lived being who they called me instead of who I really am.

I'm grateful for everything that has ever happened in my life as my past really has shaped my future. The funny thing is, even though I shouldn't have gone to jail for being in the car with my friend, I would have never gone to the halfway house, and if I'd never gone to the halfway house, I might never have discovered a part of my purpose. I'm grateful that I was able to hear from God and really put what I heard him telling me into action. I wasn't saved. I hadn't been to church; I had only been home from prison for two years. I was still in the stage of battling with the street me, the wife me, the hustler in me and humbling myself. This was a challenge, the biggest challenge ever. While I was in the halfway house, even though I was working on my purpose, I was working on getting money. I was doing things differently, getting money the legal way this time.

My wife and I had a vision to start a chicken wing business; this was more about my wife since she's a chef. I was telling my friend Unicorn, and she told me about registering the domain name and how to register the name at City Hall. We did that, and I spoke with my big homie (Hym), and he put it in my head to see about getting in a restaurant. I decided to go speak with the owner of Golden Eagle deli (Square) to see if we could we sell our wings at his location and he said "Yes." This was so exciting because it was like we were starting our own business. This brought me happiness and even caused me to put my vision on the backburner since everyone that I was asking kept telling me "No" or how it wasn't possible. I allowed this to bother me for a while; I let it bother me so much that I stopped pursuing the nonprofit. I allowed a few "Nos" to stop me. I let my love for money stop me and put all my focus on Happy Wings, which was the name of the business.

The wings were a success, and everybody from the hood was loving them. The deli was in the hood, and there were also a lot of businesses in the area. Everyone was loving Happy Wings. I would even do deliveries for orders over $25; it didn't matter what part of the city you lived in. Once the price of chicken went up, so did our prices, and that became an issue for our customers in the hood. They didn't want to pay the extra $2 that we had to charge. The customers that I didn't know paid, but the people that I knew all wanted discounts, and you can't run a successful business giving out discounts left and right. This was a cool gig while it lasted; it was perfect for me at the time because I was serving my six months in the halfway house, and this was my way out. I was able to make my own schedule for work, so I would put that I was going to work for an 8-hour shift and would only do two-three hours.

Doing this, I was able to go home a lot and see my kids when they were out of school. See, God was making a way for me through the storm; my kids had no idea I was in a halfway house. I know that would have killed my oldest son. I couldn't go back to prison this couldn't happen. I needed to figure me out and fast. My case manager in the halfway house would tell me that I was all over the place. I was trying to start my own business, working at the olive garden, running groups at the juvenile center and was trying to start a nonprofit. He told me that I needed to narrow it down. At the time, I felt he might be right, but I didn't know how to narrow it down. I had goals, and working for $13 hour wasn't one of my goals at age 32. I didn't have any understanding of how I was earning the same amount as teenagers that had an after-school or weekend job. It's like I had all this stuff going on, but it wasn't generating any money for me. Humbling myself was hard to do, accepting that pay, having a wife that made more than me, and not being able to take care of home the way I knew I was fit to do so. This was a battle that was hard for me to win. I went back and forth with myself time and time again. I knew what I needed to do, but trusting the process wasn't going to be easy.

Once I was released from the halfway house, I was able to do what I wanted to do again. I didn't have to report where I was going or when I would be back. The question is, did I learn anything about myself and who I wanted to be? I'd had six months to get my mind right and explore new business ventures. My wife had thought of another business selling kids jewelry. This was a cool idea and nobody else was doing it, plus we didn't have to spend all those hours cooking, so now we were making jewelry instead of food. The bonus for this is we have young nieces, and this would make perfect gifts for them.

So, my wife and I started selling jewelry. I'm so blessed that I have a wife that supports all that I do, and I support all that she does. We get a vision and run with it, and we're right on each other's side running; we have always been each other's #1 fan. The kid's jewelry was a success. We named it Sugamama's Vanity. Some of the jewelry we would make and some we bought already pre-made. This was fun and exciting, but the truth is, it wasn't me. It was me doing something because I didn't like working for people and getting paid chump change. I'd been a leader, with an entrepreneur mindset since I was a kid. The question is, how do I find what's really for me, and is this the one? It wasn't the one. Let me tell you something so amazing and how God leads our path with us knowing or not knowing.

One day, I was forced to return a rental car that I had been in for a few months. I couldn't afford to keep it, so it had to go back. The problem with that is I needed a car, so what was I going to do? I didn't have a driver's license or credit card, but I did have my wife's credit card and ID. Mind you, we look nothing alike; her skin tone is about three shades darker than mine. I returned the car, and now I have all this stuff with me, so I call my wife, and she goes online and makes a reservation with another car company. Now I have to see if I could get a car using my wife's information.

When I arrived at the sales counter, the lady had seemed very puzzled, and I could tell that she was struggling with something. I asked her if she was okay, and she started crying, telling me about her son, who was on drugs. She was expressing how she didn't know how to help him. She had tried everything! She'd paid for treatment, but he always used again. I told her that I work with families and provide advice, and if she wanted, I could give her my number. Mind you, at this time, I didn't have my nonprofit, and the families I was working with was my own family and friends that I would give advice to. I understood what I was like having a family member on drugs. My younger brother was struggling with fighting drug addiction, and he wouldn't listen to any of us. I did get the car, which was so odd, but it was all God; my steps were ordered.

After about a week, she called me, telling me her son was in the hospital. I told her that I was on vacation, and when I returned, I would come to see them. I went to visit him in the hospital and prayed with him. His mom was shocked because he was always so mean to everyone, even the nurses, but he was nice to me. Now let me rewind to the jewelry business. I had got an appointment to set up in front of the street board. This was a big deal, which would give me the certification that I needed to be a licensed street vendor. Now, I'd had this appointment for weeks, and I was super excited about it and then boom, I missed it because I was at the hospital with him and his mom. I didn't know these people; I had never met them before that day at the rental car place. I had never seen the son before and yet; I was at his bedside praying for him.

I wasn't a Christian or a church-going person. What is happening? How did this happen is all that I kept thinking. I was happy that I was doing something good for someone. My thing was, what about what I needed to do trying to gain financial stability for my family and me. I was so mad at myself until I saw how God was using me. Letting God in was the best thing that I could have done with my life. He gave me direction when I thought I knew the path; he sent me on a mission without me even knowing it. This was huge for me, the beginning of me understanding more about my purpose. This was God showing me the Power of Purpose. Even though I had a vision for a nonprofit and decided to stop pursuing that path, God made the path clear because this is what I was chosen to do. Could this be right for me, with all my flaws and sin? Am I supposed to lead, heal, comfort, protect and guide his people from despair?

Once I got over the shock of this, I was able to stop being mad at myself for missing something important, so I thought. What was important to me was earning income that could take care of my family, and what was important to God was me helping others and really understanding the purpose of my gift. I now understand that the person I was back then was me in the flesh, but to tap into all of me, I needed to get connected with my spirit. My flesh was leading me to self-destruction and problem after problem, while my spirit was leading me to unfamiliar places that allowed me to be free and open. Opening myself up wasn't easy; it was very hard, but once I began to open myself up and tell my story to help other people, it made my story less painful and more powerful. I was amazed at how I was able to overcome my past and how I could now use it to empower me and all those that I coach and advocate.

In that moment of needing to return that car, I was mad, frustrated, angry, and lost. I had no clue what I was going to do or how I was going to do it, but God always has a plan for us, and he's always directing us. I'm so thankful that I was able to see past being mad and decided to try for another car. I'm especially grateful that I was directed to that lady's counter. She didn't just give me a rental car that day; she helped me move one step closer to my purpose. If I hadn't been obedient at that moment, I don't know if I could depend on the Lord and his word as I do today. A lot of people never discover their purpose for many reasons. For me, I know that it was once I started to believe that I was hearing from God. If you know who you are, that's wonderful. My question is, which you do you know, the flesh you, spirit you or both? For many years, until I was 33, I only knew the Flesh me. Once I began to learn more about the spirit me, my life went in another direction, and all those different masks I used to wear were removed one mask at a time. The faith to follow God became most important, and understanding who I am became clearer.

Poem:

Understanding you or understanding me

Which one do I want to be, which one do they want to see?

My life in the bottle or my life in the sea

Nobody really knows the real me

I fight with my shadows, keeping them at the bottom of the sea

I will always wonder why God chose me

Through the sea, I am free

Through him, I am Monique

Chapter 3:

The 'Why'

This is something that I used to ask myself every time I got into trouble. I was questioning the "why." The only problem with that is I never received the answer because there was nobody that could give me an accurate answer. This was my life, actions, reactions, emotions, and feelings. The reason why I felt like this was that I had lost both my parents. The two people that taught me all that I know from what to do and what not to do. They were my everything. My mom taught me never to let a man treat me how he wants to treat me, and my dad showed me what a real man looks like who takes care of his family. My mom taught me how to break rules, and my dad taught me how to get money the legal and illegal way. My dad taught me that education is key, and my mom let me skip school when I wanted. My dad taught me to be good to people, and God will be good to you, and my mom taught me how to get over on people. My mom taught me how important family is, and my dad showed me that loving family comes with heartaches and headaches. My mom took us everywhere, showing us how to get out enjoying life, and my dad taught me how to stay home and never go anywhere with your family besides the casino or race track. My dad taught me how to buy, sell and do drugs, and my mom taught me the same thing. My dad taught me about responsibility early, adding me to his credit cards at 16, and my mom taught me how to mess my credit up, charging my cards without me or my dad knowing. My dad showed me what being in a committed relationship was like, and my mom showed me how to cheat. My dad taught me that a man should always get a blood test if in doubt, and my mom showed me what can happen when you're sleeping around with multiple guys and end up pregnant. My mom showed me unconditional love, and my dad showed me unconditional love.

My parents taught me so much, and even though I was raised with both my parents in the house, the rules and lessons along the way were very different. One minute, there were rules, and the next minute, I was able to do what I wanted. I think a big part of this was because they didn't really know who their baby girl was. The little girl Monique was very sweet, loving, charming and caring to everyone, but she had an evil side about her, and then there was the tomboy. I lived with the tomboy for most of my life; the tomboy helped keep the fast girl hidden so that nobody would know about her. See, that's what a lot of people do—cover up who they really are to be the person that fits with what everyone else wants for them. I'm a witness that living like that will never allow you to discover you. Growing up, I didn't question my parents about their parenting style; I did what I was told, and I was sneaky when it came to doing things I wasn't supposed to do.

Don't get me wrong; there were times when I would ask "why" I had to do something or "why" I had to go somewhere. The problem with that is the answer to my "why" was always lined up with their perspective on things and not mine. So now I'm older and want answers to "why" I am the way I am and "why" I behaved the way I behaved as a kid. Why do I have the friends I have? Why did I choose the woman I chose to marry? Why did I go to prison? Why am I so skinny? Why can't I gain weight? Why do I have to be so mean? Why do I have to always be in control? Why did I have to sell drugs? Why did I have to leave my son? Why did I choose to be in a same-sex relationship? Why didn't I graduate from college? Why didn't I discover my purpose sooner? Why did I feel that I had to be a cheater because I was cheated on? Why do I pray with people I don't know? Why do I write books? Why do I have to do a million things at once? Why do I have dogs? Why do I like running the show? Why can't I sit still? Why is it hard for me to listen? Why do I talk so much? And the why can go on and on. But I'm going to show you how getting answers to some of these "why's" is what helped me understand who I was, what direction I wanted my life to go in, what I needed to stop doing and who I needed to remove from my life in order to live the life that I was visioning in my head.

Knowing the "Why" is knowing you and when you know you, the battle is won and living the victory begins. So, let's start with some of my "Whys." Why do I behave the way that I did before I knew my why? That came from a lot of trauma that was covered up when I was a child, the things that happened to me, being violated and the things that were happening around me, drug use, drug sales, police kicking in our door, and then there's' the life of growing up in the projects. I was exposed to so much at a young age, but that was normal in my neighborhood; it wasn't something that was being talked about as if it was a problem. You knew better than to go to school and tell the staff anything about what was going on in the house. That was rule #1. Never tell anyone about nothing at home, if the school called and said you'd been talking about what your parents did to you, it was going to happen ten times worse. This was even a rule that I lived by when my son started going to school, which is not a good rule to go by all the time. I feel that it forces kids to keep things bottled up and doing that only affects them in the long run, either as a teen, young adult or adult. Now, I don't worry about these things with my youngest kids and the reason why is that I'm a different parent now. The same behavior they were taught as kids is the same behavior they have as adults, I know this is what happened for me. Instead of seeing that everything I was dealing with and going through was wrong, it was just considered another day in the hood.

I was taught to keep secrets at a young age from my mom, which is why I believe I became sneaky, trying to get away with all types of things. I didn't know my "why" to this behavior before, but I do now. I would go to Safeway every morning with my cousins to steal candy so that I could have a party in my classroom. Now, why was I doing this because it was learned behavior; I had seen my mom steal before and get away with it, so I thought I could do the same thing. My teacher told me that I couldn't eat candy in the class unless I brought enough for everyone. I did just that: I made sure I got candy for everyone. This lasted for a few months until I was caught stealing and couldn't go back into that Safeway. My parents weren't called, so they had no idea what I was doing or that I had been caught.

My problem was I liked to break the rules. Why is that? Because as a little girl, my mother showed me how to break rules; she showed me how to get what you want without paying for it. Don't be silly and think she said, "Monique, this is what you do when you want to steal." She didn't do that; she just did it around me, and I was very observant, watching her every move. Therefore, it's very important to be careful about what you introduce your kids to and what you don't. Just because you think they're not watching or listening means most of the time, they are. I never took anything when I was with my mom; I would be too scared of what she would do if I got caught, but when she wasn't around, I did everything that I had no business doing. I had this type of behavior because I'd seen my mom get away with things when nobody was looking. I know she wasn't trying to teach me that, but that's the problem when you are a kid; you're not just listening to what you're being told; you are observing everything that happens around you. Like we used to say, "soaking up all the game."

That's the reality of it, and that's why you're not supposed to talk around kids. My parents sent us to the other room a lot, but I didn't care about that. I would come out for something to drink or to use the bathroom. This is what I did to listen to what our parents were talking about. The only time I wanted to listen is when they had company and weren't talking to me. Then there's the "why" you choose the relationships you choose. That all comes from your past, how you were loved, were both parents in the home, and how your extended family behaved towards you. What does love look like and feel like for you? How you love yourself and your need to be loved. When you have a need to be loved, you accept more of what a person is telling you, instead of showing you. Even when their actions aren't aligned with their words, "I Love You." Dig deep under the surface of your self-needs, wants and desires when it comes to what real love looks like for you.

Why was I a fast-little girl that nobody knew about? This has always been a question that I had, and now I know the answer as I look back on the little girl me; the girl that wore a mask and the girl that needed Mone. Maybe, if I wasn't violated as a kid, then I wouldn't have had these secret relations, but since a little girl, I was shown how to keep secrets. I was touched in secret, so this was normal for me. This really traumatized me, and I had no clue about this until I found God, and now I'm scared for all little girls being alone with men, on their laps, changing their diapers, kissing them on the lips, being in swimsuits at the pool without shorts on top. I shouldn't feel this way, but I do because of my past issues. Just think if God would have given me a girl? I might have traumatized her with all my insecurities about men. Why was this my way of thinking? Why did I have to go through this? These are answers that I will never get answered; I will forever be in the dark.

No child should feel that it's normal to be violated, but if you can't trust the adults in your life, who can you trust? It makes me so mad that I will never be able to ask the people that did this to me. I wonder, did he ever have any regrets about the things that he did to me? I wonder if he did this to other family members? I will never get those answers. I will keep his name sealed because he's gone home with the Lord. I do know that I wasn't the only one that drove on his lap. I know that he did this to other family members. What I don't know is if they feel that they were violated. Could me being violated have something to do with, "why" I chose the men I chose? Looking back, I think it was about security. It was about me feeling safe with them; therefore, I needed someone that had a reputation in the streets and not a square guy. All the past trauma that I faced and my need for protection. I wasn't in any danger, so why did I need protection? I needed protection from myself and all the private thoughts that drove me crazy. I was loved by both my parents; they showed me perfect love as I know it. That came with a few ass whippings, and a bunch of other things that would make a kid like me get mad with my parents and my parents get frustrated with me.

When I was 11 years old, I ran away. I didn't go far, but that's not the point. At 11, I thought it was okay to leave my house and act like I wasn't going back because my dad took my pager from me, and I wanted it back. He didn't pay for it, so why should he keep it? This is what I was feeling at the time. I went to my friend's house in the other court; our projects were built like a square cut into five parallel pieces. My friend lived in the second court, and I lived in the first court. It was normal for me to go to her house, so her mom had no problem with me being there. Everyone kept telling me that my mom was worried, so I called home and talked to my mom. She said, "baby come home; you can have your pager, just come home, I love you." We said some other things, and then I went home. My dad gave me my pager, and we didn't talk about it. See, he was in his mode, getting high, so he wasn't worried about me now, but when that high came down, it was another story.

My parents didn't speak with me about my behavior when it was bad; I was either getting a whopping or yelled at. I wasn't getting a sit-down to discuss the who, what, where, when and why? I know that if my parents had taken the time out to discuss things like this, I would've been more self-aware of my behavior. Most of the time, they overlooked the things that I did and said. This showed me "Why" I let a lot of things go that my kids do when, in reality, I'm only hurting them in the long run by not teaching them about consequences for their actions. Maybe if my parents had been stricter with punishing me, I would have understood that I couldn't get away with everything. When your mindset is focused on what you can get instead of what you can give, that means you're more in the flesh and not the spirit.

My wife also grew up in a loving household where it was dinner at the table, chores to be done, weekend parties with adults and the kids serving food and drinks, family outings, family gatherings and so much more. This is where we vibe at; this is how we relate to each other amongst other things. Then there are the similarities in things like humping girls as a kid, being gifted in the spirit and being scared as a kid, and most importantly, knowing how to love each other with unconditional love. From day #1, I knew she was the beginning of a faithful, committed relationship, and the last because we would marry and spend the rest of our lives together. My wife and I were dealing with so much trauma that we couldn't love everyone before us, and they couldn't love us because neither one of us knew who we were. The mask was our shield from facing our ugly truth. Even though I had been through therapy multiple times, every day for years because it was offered in the drug program in prison. The program helped me to be released six months early. However, none of it worked because I was never forced to see who Monique really was. I didn't get the chance to remove the mask; nobody got below the surface. It was all about whatever I wanted to share. It didn't matter if it was bullshit or not, they didn't know, and they didn't care enough to see past it.

So, now I'm blessed with my wife, someone who accepts me with all my flaws and vice versa. We loved each other since day #1. She supports my visions, takes care of home, loves my family, loves my son like her own, and most importantly, loves me with no limits. Through our years of growing and trying to learn about each other, we started to learn more about ourselves because habits that caused pain in previous relationships weren't working in this one. That learned behavior of using words to hurt the one you love because I'm hurt wasn't working. I had to dig deep and revamp the old Monique to a new Monique, and that's exactly what happened; without therapy, we were able to be each other's therapist. We started to reveal things to each other that we had never shared before and instead of us using it against each other in a later argument, we counseled one another, being there to listen, a shoulder to cry on, being what we needed to be for each other. Being able to be real with each other really opened old wounds that were buried way down. I always thought I was handling things and was soon hit with reality. I was hurting my wife and wasn't conscious of it.

Why was this happening? Because it was the only way that I knew how to communicate when I was mad; it was the only way I knew how to communicate if I wanted to make the other person mad. Before this, I would always work out in my favor, not with my wife. She wasn't going for that type of mental abuse, and I didn't want to lose her. So, I made the shifts in my mind that I needed to make in order to stop causing my wife pain and going through the same thing over and over again. This makes me think about why I was choosing the type of people I was choosing to be with before her. I know now that I was choosing people that fit my image instead of people that were good for my spirit.

When I was younger, my relationships really didn't have the value that they should have had in my life; I was just doing something. I was basically passing time and getting the person that fit my street image. This is exactly why me and them never worked out. Why do I have the friends I have? All my friends are the same people that I grew up with my whole life. I never cared for new friends; I was the type of person that felt that you couldn't trust new people in your circle as this could cause problems, but that's not my mindset anymore. Now, I feel that I need to meet new people; new people are good as they can help me elevate. You never know who's part of your purpose, so don't be scared to let people in otherwise you could miss out on a big opportunity. I know I've missed plenty of opportunities because of my pride and stubborn ways. I look back on my old ways and kick myself in the butt because I know that I've dropped the ball, not knowing my "Why." All my old friends fit my old life; some fit my new life, and some didn't. This has been the hard part about stepping into my purpose and knowing my "Why." Now that I'm learning more about my "Why," I know all my friends are my friends because of my old lifestyle. The question is, how do we move forward? Can they accept me, and can I accept them for who we are now?

The "Why" to my childhood friends is just that; they were from my childhood. Do I know the 'Why' when it comes to my adult friends? Friendships are supposed to be valuable; they're supposed to be joined with someone that you can lean on when things are difficult, the shoulder you can cry on when you're feeling down. They give you good advice when you're feeling confused, and most importantly, their loyalty is always with you, especially when it comes to outsiders. Friendships like this make the "Why" easy, but when you have to question the "Why," and you can't really answer that, then it might not be a friendship worth keeping. Don't hold on to any relationships when you can't answer the "Why" with confidence. Always take time and reevaluate your relationships and make sure they still line up with your life. The worst thing you can do is keep people around just because of the years you've known each other. Sometimes, you must deal with a person from afar, and sometimes, you must cut them off completely.

Let's talk about the "Why" do I work where I work

and how does this job line up with my purpose? I used to always quit every job I had in a year; it didn't matter how much money I was making; I would always quit. I would always find happiness in any job that I was doing, but I couldn't find enough comfort to stay. When I came home from prison, I was blessed with a really good job, Stationary Engineer. It was good pay, starting at $26hr and maxed out at $60hr in four years, once I finished school. I did that job for three months, and then I was fired because I didn't put the correct social security number on the paper. What was my "Why" for this behavior? I didn't have faith in God the way that I do now, and that cost me my job. Most importantly, it taught me that I would always lose that battle without faith and putting God in all that I do. For months, I was so mad at myself. Now I was unemployed, had bills and my son to take care of, and at the time, I was only dating my wife, so all these problems were my problems alone.

Because I was in the union, I was still able to get sent out on interviews for the same position, which I was happy about. I knew I had to trust God and be honest about my past record moving forward. Every interview went well, and they all liked me; the problem is, none of them hired me. I was forced to take a job working with my sister and not making very much money, making half of what I was making at first. I would still go out and get money the illegal way, so taking a pay cut was fine. I had to have a job to report to my probation officer. About a year went by, and I went on about seven interviews, but they all went with someone else. I knew this was God because I had watched TD. Jakes on TV that same weekend that I was fired. He was talking about how God showed Moses the land and told him it could be his. At that moment, he wasn't ready, but he had to go through the process, and I knew this message was for me. God was directing all that was happening to me. I knew he was testing my faith; this is what I kept telling myself.

I continued to believe. At this time, my wife and I were together. We were no longer with other people, so she was also a part of this process with me. When I look back at that job and ask 'Why,' it was all about the money and the stability it would have brought my son and me. It had good benefits and something that everyone works for, the big retirement package. I'm grateful that it was all part of my growing process and I didn't get stuck there, because for a minute I did. It was all I could think about and more because I went on seven more interviews for the same job, and I didn't get it. That process grew my faith in God, and I knew that everything I was going through was part of the setup for the promise ahead. Don't get me wrong; this was no easy task, and it caused me many sleepless nights, arguments with myself and insecurities within. This was a battle that I knew I had to win. I knew the enemy was trying to keep me down. He didn't want to see me win; he wanted me to keep questioning the "Why" instead of knowing the "Why."

The more time that passed, my wife and I began to grow as a unit, and that job became something less desirable to me. I was focused on making my nonprofit, which was super exciting and frustrating. Why was I having this vision, and was this the journey for me? When I replay my childhood in my head, it was like "Yes," this is for me; this is it. I was hit with so much opposition after the vision that I couldn't focus on the vision. I had to focus on making a living to support my family because now it was me, my wife and our three sons. My wife had a great job; she worked at PG&E making $50hr, which was enough to take care of us, but me being me, I didn't feel good about that. Then came the "Why Me?" Why is this happening to me? Why don't I have a good job? Why can't I pay for us to go out on dates? Why do I have to ask her for money when she gets paid?

The why never stopped because I was unhappy within, and I kept making my wife the problem when she was the solution for our family at that moment. She never made me feel bad about not being able to provide the way she was, but my insecurities made me feel some type of way. Instead of working hard on the vision, I started working hard on the hustle. I had to show her that I could take care of this family and all I was doing was putting us in a deeper hole day by day doing illegal activities. Instead of seeing her as being able to take care of the home as a bonus for our family, I saw it as a problem, and then I created a bigger problem for us because now some of that illegal activity had caught up with me. So now it was the "Why Me" again. Why did I have to fight another case? Was I going to prison? Was I going to leave my wife and kids? I will tell you why.

The problem again was I didn't trust God to supply all my needs; I kept feeling like I had to do it. I needed to do things my way; I needed to do what I knew best, and that was hustling for money. The problem then, and the problem now with getting money is that I didn't acknowledge God at that time. I didn't seek him or really know him, and now I do. Just as it's written he will never forsake me, he just sent me through test after test, and this was going to be the final test for me when it came to illegal hustling. I kept asking "Why," and every time, the answer was the same. My lack of faith in him, my lack of trust in God, my pride of having to always fix something and my stubbornness in feeling like I must be in control. I was my biggest battle, and until I really understood that, I would keep being knocked down. If I had trusted God and put all my faith in him as I was doing when I was going on those job interviews, then maybe I wouldn't be in this same situation fighting a case and possibly going to prison. This was so heartbreaking to me; I felt like a failure. How was I going to tell my son, who was now 13, that his mom had to go back to jail? I had only been home for two years.

I was so mad at myself. I knew better than to keep hustling, but I thought I would be okay since they didn't have anything solid. Not everybody can be trusted, and I found out the hard way once again. The person that was working for me snitched, and there it is; they had a case. Everything inside of me wanted to flash, fight and everything else, but where was that going to get me? In jail. I let her know that I knew she'd snitched, and I hoped she wouldn't take the stand because I was taking this all the way to trial. They offered me four years, and after two years of fighting the case, I was blessed with a great sentence, nine months in the halfway house in Redwood City. Then there came the "Why" am I back in the halfway house only this time on house arrest? I only had to do check-ins.

This was a part of my journey. Even though I wasn't obedient, God was still directing my steps, making the "Why" clear to everything that I was going through, and if the "Why" wasn't clear, then I knew I didn't need to worry about it. I'm the type of person who's always searching for the "Why," and I think this helped me stay focused on the journey ahead. It opened my eyes to situations that I might have stayed asleep on. When you're searching for your "Why," don't run to people, run to God, run to the holy spirit for answers because nobody can answer your "Why." The answer to your "Why" is closer than you think, but if you don't search for it, then how can you grow into your authentic self? Trust in you, trust in the process and trust in your "Why."

If I had got stuck in the "Why" in that situation and made it personal, I wouldn't have been able to forgive the girl that snitched on me. And if I hadn't forgiven her, then I might have been serving that four years in jail, instead of nine months on house arrest. You might be asking "Why" do I think that? I know in my heart that it was a test from God; I know that he used her and that situation to strengthen me and teach me a lesson. I had to learn that it was my crime, and when you do the crime, you do the time. I found purpose in every bad situation that I went through, and doing this has brought me peace and happiness. I'm so in love with the Power of Purpose. It has blessed me to be open-minded to people and their current situations. Just because I understand my "Why" doesn't mean that the person involved with me understands their "Why." Because of that, I must always remind myself that the "Why" is Never Personal, Always Purpose.

Poem:

Why do I do the things I do?

Why do I never see the real you?

Why is the question, and sometimes, I ask Who?

Who is the reason behind my behavior?

Who is the one that gives me favor?

Who taught me how to forgive?

The man above, who shows me love

I'm forever grateful and thankful for his hug

Chapter 4
In the Midst of it

When you're in the midst of the chaos, your thinking can be off. Instead of being logical and trying to see the purpose behind what is going on, you make it personal. Often, this can cause a bigger problem. Think about what you gain when you take things personally. When you are in a heated situation, it is best to step back, give yourself time to cool down, rethink the situation and try to figure out where the issue began and how it can be resolved. Most of the time, problems start from an unreasonable attempt at effective communication. You cannot expect a person to be ready to communicate when they're mad or frustrated. It is during this time when everybody should respect each other's personal space. It's important to know your boundaries in the midst of heated situations, especially if you're dealing with someone that you don't know because the outcome is unpredictable. Let me tell you about a few of my situations where I was in the midst of the chaos and how it worked out when I took it personally versus how it worked out when I learned how to see the purpose, its power in discovering your purpose.

The first situation was a fight between my parents when I was seven years old. My mom was hitting my dad, and my dad kept trying to get out of the house. Finally, he was able to get out, but she kept following him. Once he got down the stairs, she stopped because they were outside, and everyone was watching. I don't know what they were fighting about, but I do know my dad never hit my mom. He taught us that men don't hit women. My mom went back into the house, yelling to my dad to get all his things. He ignored her and continued his way to the store. My daddy loved to go to the store to gamble as he liked to play the poker machine. Even though they were arguing, I was never afraid of my dad leaving. My mom liked to yell at my dad when he wouldn't do what she wanted. Even though I know my daddy ran the household, it was really like my mom did. She was the boss; he was the provider.

In the middle of that chaos, both my parents taught me two valuable lessons: don't ever bring your business out in the streets, and a man should never hit a woman. My daddy knew to never take things personally with my mom. She was stubborn and, more importantly, she was a Gemini, with switch personalities. One minute, she would be good, and within a blink of an eye, it would be all bad. Instead, my dad focused on the purpose, taking everything my mom dished out in order to take care of my siblings and I. He loved my mom very much; he didn't say it all the time, but he showed it. My daddy taught me early on that I didn't need to fight every battle and it's not about who tells you they love you, it's about who shows you. But, of course, I wasn't paying attention to that part.

In my past relationships, I took everything personally. It was always a problem. When I was with my son's father and another dude, boy, was that terrible for me. See, when you're trying to figure out your feelings, everyone in the midst of the chaos gets hurt. I was torn between two men. This was the first time in my life that I was in love with two people...so I thought. What I know now is that I was in love with the fact that they both were fighting over me, and I was not letting anybody have my ex unless I wanted them to. The sad part is that their fighting was an infatuation of mine. It made me feel good, but all the while, it was hurting them. By allowing this to continue, I was also selfish in failing to acknowledge that because they were both from the street, it could have ended way worse than just fighting. Someone could have gotten shot.

I'm so grateful that God made sure that everyone stayed safe. I was really playing with fire. I knew that my current boyfriend was insecure about my ex and vice versa. But instead of leaving one alone, I would always run to the other when one would make me mad. I was making it very personal. I knew I didn't want my ex back; that's why he was an ex. The problem was, I didn't want anybody else to have him. I knew that I could always have him by getting with him again, just to prove that I could. This was how crazy my mind used to be. I wanted to keep dealing with a man just to show another woman that I could always have him. This was so silly and could have turned out really badly.

I'm glad I got over that silly stuff. I never knew what the purpose was then. Looking back, I would say the purpose was to prepare me for helping young ladies that struggle with the same kind of insecurities that I had. I didn't know how to overcome this issue when I was in the midst of it, but now I do, as I have acquired the tools needed to deal with this type of mindset. I also realize that some of my insecurities caused me to have a destructive mindset. I also believe it came from the domestic violence I was a witness to. I was slapped by my mom so much, I grew up thinking that was love. If I was with a man that didn't want to call me a "Bitch" or hit me when I would get smart with him, he wasn't good enough for me. What in the world was I thinking? I wasn't! I was used to what I had seen growing up and what I was seeing in the midst of things. My daddy called everybody a "Bitch." He didn't say it mean or disrespectful; it was like a term of endearment for him. Everybody on the block used that word, including me. I used it in every sentence. It was my normal. I would even call boys, "Bitch." Early on, I was taught that this was okay, so when I would get slapped... we 'd have sex after that. How twisted was that line of thinking?

This wasn't just my normal; this was the normal in the neighborhood. It was nothing for your boyfriend to beat you up and y'all still be together. Many little girls today are witnesses to physical and mental abuse in their everyday life, be it home, stores, restaurants, or schools. The problem I have with this is, just as I didn't know to speak up and speak out in the midst of the chaos, I would assume that they don't know how to deal with this either. Many of us grow up thinking that what we believe to be normal, okay or right, in reality, could all be wrong. Most of my life, I lived with things that weren't right, but because it was the normal in my environment, it was okay. My mom hit me, and it was okay; my boyfriend hit me, and it was okay; if I didn't get hit, it wasn't okay. Every day, I witnessed a woman or child be hit, and this was normal in my environment.

Sometimes, I think about how my life would be had I grown up in a different environment, especially given the knowledge and perspective I have now, but then again, I also know that if anything about my childhood would have been different, then I wouldn't be who I am today. That could be a good thing or a bad thing, but it's something that I will never find out. I'm grateful for the woman that God blessed me to grow into. All the pain, trauma, confusion, heartbreak, loneliness, and despair were intended to set me up for this moment right here, the writing of this book.

When I was struggling with how to live the street life and live the family life at the same time, I was on a rollercoaster ride that was doing more turns than I could handle. The problem was that I couldn't see or didn't want to see what was really going on. When my wife would get up to go to work, I would get up with her, even though I didn't have a job. Most of the time, I didn't do anything, except hang out on the block. After a while, that got old. I would look for a job, but I couldn't find a position that paid enough for me. Instead of settling for what was available, I would rather try to get money by hustling. I must be honest, though, I did end up with a few odd jobs before finding my purpose. I was a delivery driver, delivering coffee. That was a cool gig because I worked alone all day, and I liked to drive. This also gave me time with my sister, which was an obvious plus. But being who I was, I wasn't happy with this job because it didn't pay enough. My wife was making more than me, and I didn't like it.

Being so ambitious definitely motivates me to always push harder. This character trait has also been my downfall, as I am never satisfied. When I was arrested for drugs, I finally realized that I couldn't keep dealing. I had to do something because hustling was in me, so I started boosting. For those that don't know what that is, boosting is a term used for stealing out of the stores. I was pretty good at getting whatever I wanted, mostly clothes because I could sell them in the hood. Boosting was a rush. We would go in those stores, grab some stacks and run out. I remember this one time me, my twin, and Our Angel (Sheda) were in Berkeley, boosting from Mr. Rags. Back then, Mr. Rags was the spot. They had all the name brand clothes that the rappers were wearing, like Roc A Wear, Akademiks, and Sean John. That's what was hot in the early 2000s. We went in there grabbing stacks. We ran to the car and thought we'd got away.

As we were driving, we pulled up to a light, and my twin and I switched places; I went to the passenger seat, and my twin became the driver. As soon as we did, we noticed the police were to the right of us. Our light turned green, and as we proceeded to go, he made a right turn getting behind us. A few seconds later, he turned his lights on and pulled us over. He then asked twin for her insurance and license. I remember Sheda saying, "I can't go back to that group home" and twin just hit the gas. The officer went running back to his car, but he was too slow. Twin was gone. She ran the lights, went to the side, and then faked him and got on the freeway. We took the long way back to the city, across the San Mateo bridge just in case the highway patrol was waiting at the bay bridge. I was about 21 years old.

Here I am, fighting a case, risking it all, and for what? I'm out here taking chances with my life and then began to think, 'Where is my son? Why am I not with him? What's going to happen if we get caught? What the hell am I going to do?' Interestingly, as soon as we got away with it, all those thoughts went out of my mind just as quickly as they came in. When we didn't get caught, I didn't care about it anymore. Now in the midst of it, all I could think about was my son and what I would do if God got me out of this situation, and as soon as he got me out, I went right back to it.

Back then, I didn't believe in God the way I do now, and I didn't really care about what my parents were talking about because I was grown. During this time, my parents were still alive. All the while, they were the ones looking out for my son while I was being young and dumb, running the streets. When I was in the midst of things, and God got me out of a bad situation, I didn't care to see the lesson behind it; I just considered everything luck. I was 'lucky' time and time again. I'm so grateful that God always got me out of bad situations, and even though I didn't give him the glory, I know without a doubt that it was him now. I was good at putting myself in bad situations.

There was a time when I had a hard time being exclusive. I knew that I should have stopped dealing with Her once I got with my wife. I knew that there was no way that I could continue to play both sides of the game, but because I needed money and wanted to get it the easy way, I continued to use Her to get the numbers I needed to do credit card fraud. That got me the money I wanted in the moment, but this is the case that landed me on house arrest after serving my six-month violation in the halfway house. When the police went to her job questioning her, she gave me up. I was so mad at first, but how could I be mad? I knew that she had mixed feelings because we had something going on in the past, and then I ended it because of my wife. At that point, all I wanted were the numbers.

What I didn't understand in the midst of all this is that I was using her. I jeopardized her job, freedom, and integrity. This isn't something she was doing because she wanted to; this is something she was doing because I introduced her to this lifestyle. She loved me and was willing to do anything I wanted to spend time with me. Of course, in the beginning, it didn't start like that because she was my ex-girlfriend, so we were both benefiting each other. Even though I was honest with her about having a new girlfriend, it was still wrong of me. She wasn't the only one either, the girl that was going into the stores for me using the cards even gave me up. I can remember when a problem would arise; I would blame the person that I felt caused the problem instead of seeing what role I'd played in it. As they say, you get older and wiser. Now I'm wiser, and as I look back, I feel bad for some of the things I've done as a person, sister, mother, friend, girlfriend, and cousin.

When we were fighting the case, I knew I had to forgive them both if I wanted to receive my blessings. I talked with both of them, and I told the girl getting the numbers that I understood her position. I forgave her, and I hoped that she could forgive me. I also let her know that I couldn't be her friend anymore, but I could release all negative feelings that I was feeling towards her and the situation so that I could move on with my life and she could move on with hers. This wasn't easy, especially since I did have feelings for her; we'd been girlfriends for a few years, and even though I had moved on, I always felt that we would be able to remain friends. When I was in the midst of it, I only wanted to see my side. I had to think outside the box and see that I'd really hurt her and that it was my wants and needs that got us here. Yes, she made a choice to do it or not, but if I hadn't given her that choice, we would have never had to fight that case and do time. I was able to see the lesson for me, and I prayed that she was able to see the lesson for her. The crazy thing about that is she had to do a federal violation and state time. I received a better deal, and I didn't snitch.

The other girl and I had known each other since we were kids; my mom used to watch her. I couldn't believe she snitched! I knew her parents, so I went to her dad and told him about her snitching, and he assured me that I didn't have anything to worry about. When I went to court and saw her there, it made me so mad because she acted like it was all good, and she hadn't done anything. In the midst of it, I wanted to do so much. I wanted to blast her on social media, fight her, and do everything I could to expose her. Once again, God let me know that we all must pay for our actions, and she would pay for hers. It might not be with jail, but it would be with something and maybe 10x worst.

The lesson I learned from this was to never do crime with anyone other than myself. I learned never to do crime, and I wouldn't have to do the time. I learned not to put myself in situations with people that could possibly have me arrested. I learned that just because they hurt you doesn't mean they won't hurt worse. I learned to sit back and observe more and avoid people that need. I learned that when I forgive, I'm in control. Forgiving them was good for my soul; it wasn't about being good for them. When you decide to forgive someone or say "sorry," you don't have to feel weak or like a sucker. Being the bigger person is good; it's about taking your power back and not allowing yourself to have all those head trips about what could've, should've, would've happened. When I was in the midst of a family battle, I didn't understand what was going on and why it was happening. Back in my old neighborhood, I knew of these sisters who loved each other very much; it was very clear. It was also clear that the older sister was jealous of the younger sister. The problem with that is the younger sister didn't know it, and she looked up to the older sister, always wanting to do what she was doing, wearing makeup like her and just always trying to be like her. This became clear to me when I started hanging around them more, so I brought it up with the younger sister, and she began to pay attention.

On this one particular day, everyone was having a good time, and the sisters start arguing and fighting about things that happened in the past. The older sister got mad at the younger sister for not really understanding all the things that happened when they were kids. She didn't like that the younger sister didn't see anything wrong with what had happened to them. Even though they both went through getting whippings, being yelled at, having things thrown at them and so much more, the younger sister had learned to move on and forgive her parents while the older sister wasn't so forgiving. In the midst of everything, it was bad, and both girls felt like they were in a nightmare, but now it's behind them, and in order to be free from all that trauma they both faced as young girls, they both have to forgive. Because the older sister won't forgive, she has made her life difficult when it comes to love, trust, relationships, and her emotions. She had been used to not talking about it, lashing out as a sign of help, but nobody paid attention to her behavior. She was considered a troubled girl, but that still didn't prompt anyone to get her help either. What's funny is the little sister is the one that got help; she had a therapist. It was for something different, but she had one, and I believe that's why she was able to let go and forgive quicker than her sister. The older sister would do mean things to the little sister, push her down the stairs, put a pillow over her head, write on her face, and always lie on her. It was pretty bad, and even though they can look back on this now, they're both still dealing with the trauma that happened to them as kids because, in the midst of it, nobody came to their rescue.

At this point, they can only rescue each other by being very honest about their childhood and the impact it has had on their adult life. What the older sister doesn't realize is her anger towards her parents has affected her parenting. I don't think we as parents fully realize the effect that we have on our kids when it comes to what we do, the environment we raise them in, what we expose them to, and how we respond to them. These sisters dealt with a lot as children, and because all they had was each other, they took their problems out on each other. The problem with that is that if you never talk about it and understand what happened and why, how can you really move forward having unconditional love? No doubt, it's hard to do. I think when you've been hurt multiple times by an adult that you trust like a parent, your older sibling becomes your protector in your mind, and then when you get older, you realize that they were never protecting you, and, in fact, caused you more harm ...it can be traumatizing. It can keep you stuck in the past, stuck in the problem, especially if you haven't grown mentally to realize that a lot of things that happened to us as kids can be out of our control.

If you don't have someone helping you overcome some of the obstacles as they come up, you can't get past them. Now everyone in the family is infected like the flu. Everybody is in the midst of it. Taking sides and adding their two cents-creating a bigger problem instead of trying to figure out the root. When you have fights with your siblings or family members when you're younger, it's overlooked. Everyone acts as if, "oh, they're just kids," when the reality is, they are kids with issues. Kids need someone to talk to about what they're experiencing. I know that these things were overlooked for me, and I know that they've been overlooked for a lot of the people I coach. I don't think it's overlooked on purpose. It happens because of the way you were raised, your parents were raised and how their parents were raised. What issues they addressed and what issues they swept under the rug.

If I knew then what I know now, I would be in a different situation. I didn't say better because I didn't know better, but I do know different. If I had learned how to manage my money the way my daddy was trying to show me at a young age instead of spending it all in the midst of living a carefree hustling lifestyle, I would have more than I have today. That carefree "I don't care. I'm going to do what I wanna do" attitude didn't do anything but provide me with lesson after lesson. The problem with that is when I was in the midst of it, I wasn't really learning the lesson; I was just going with the flow. Before I went to federal prison, I had been in and out of jail at least six times. Every time I went to jail, it was always for something adjacent to the real crime, never for what I really did. I think that might be the reason I never learned the lesson that God was trying to teach me. I feel I know the lesson today. I would go to jail and bail out or wait the 72 hours. This way, I wouldn't have to pay because 95% of the time, they would let me out. If I had learned that selling drugs, boosting, check fraud and credit card fraud was causing me more harm than good, I would have quit a long time ago. However, I was so busy being in the midst of everything that I kept missing a valuable lesson, and that lesson was to stop. I didn't take heed to God locking me up as a sign to do better. I saw it as a sign to tighten my game up.

See, this thinking all came from my childhood, from what I had seen and how nobody had ever guided me towards a different path. My daddy always talked to me about a different path, but how do you really want something different when the people you love and look up to are living according to the environment? My daddy was trying to tell me to do things in a certain way, but his words didn't line up with his actions. He was doing the same things that he was telling me not to do, but all I saw was what was happening in the hood. Since his job was out of state, most of the time, I didn't see him interact with business people or people out-side our community. I know that if I had seen him in action, I would have been sharper than an electric knife.

Instead, he was showing me how to survive in my neighborhood. Just as my house would get raided when I was a kid and my parents went back to doing what they were doing, not fazed by all the chaos happening to them in our home or outside our home; I too continued to move on with business as usual amidst my own chaos. I know my parents would love the opportunity to tell me their side on why they kept dealing drugs and doing drugs after our house was raided. I hated being questioned by the neighborhood and police about what my parents were doing. I never had the answers, and they never told us anything besides, "it's none of their business." When my mom got the opportunity to move to another city, she did. My dad didn't move with my mom right away; he didn't want to live in the country (as he called Pittsburg). He felt that he left Mississippi to get away from the county, and he wasn't going back. He never went back to Mississippi for family reunions or Thanksgiving and because of this (as a child), I never went either. I al-ways wanted to stay with my dad.

When my mom moved, I took over our old house. Now I was in a 3-bedroom project house with just me and my baby; my son was a few months old during this time. My lit-tle brother moved in with me and then just as my parents had the dope house, my house became the dope hallway. I didn't make sells in my house, but I would go in the hallway to make sells while my son was in his swing or playpen. This was terrible, but when I was in the midst of it, I didn't see anything wrong with it. This was my normal. So many things were my normal that I know were wrong, which could have turned out badly for me. If the police came in my hallway, I would've gone to jail and my son to CPS. I'm so grateful that God chose my son and me every time. My son could've been taken away from me at a young age because of my carefree behavior and doing what I had seen my parents do. I know that my parents wanted the best for all of us. They wanted us to get out of the hood and be the best we could be. My older sister went the right way. She didn't sell drugs; she worked since she was 14. I also worked since I was 14. We had summer jobs when we were teens in our neighborhood.

I wondered why I couldn't just do right? Why did I have to be like my parents? My answer then would have been because I am my parents. Now, I realize that as much as I was a leader, I was also a follower. I was too busy following what I was seeing instead of being the leader that God designed me to be. I didn't have to stay in the midst of things, but I did. I chose to do what everybody else was doing. I wanted the fast money, cars, clothes and the street guy. When you're in the midst of your situation, it's hard to see a clear path; it's hard to hear from God and follow His steps. If you're anything like I was, please look back at your life and really begin to analyze where you became the person you're today. Everything we go through is a life lesson and meant to make us stronger, but sometimes, we can put ourselves in situations over and over again to the point that it drains everything out of you, and you can't see anything but the current and past pain. You can't see the future; you can't see the purpose. Instead, you make it personal and all about you when none of it's about you. It's not even happening to you; it's happening through you and for you to gain a stronger perspective. This strength will allow you to deal with something like this again or help someone that might be dealing with the same thing.

I didn't know how to think clearly when I was in the midst of things going bad; all I could do was hurry up and try to fix it. Trying to fix it most of the time only made it worse for me in the long run. When I would get my car towed because I was driving with a suspended license, I didn't stop driving to work on getting my license back. I would go find someone who could get me a rental car. That was a good fix in the midst of it, but in the long run, all it did was cost me more money. I was paying $350 a week, $250 for the car and a $100 fee to the person that was renting me the car. I had no license and drove like I was a Nascar driver. I got pulled over a lot. When I got pulled over, the police would take the car. As a result, I was stuck paying $1,000 in fines. This happened to me many times, but I never learned my lesson. I was too busy caught up in the idea of being 'that girl' with money, cars, and clothes.

I was worried about everything that shouldn't have mattered to me. I should have been worried about my son and saving money for him to go to college. But no, that was the least of my worries. I was young and dumb and more focused on him looking fresh in the streets. My son is my world and has been since he was in my belly. I'm so mad at myself for not making better decisions as his mother. I can remember fighting with people from my block, and then everything would be back to normal because somebody would intervene and make sure things didn't stay a problem. The older generation kept the younger generation in line, but this doesn't happen anymore. Now, everyone is worried about the problem instead of trying to find a solution. Instead of stepping back, everyone wants to take a step forward, being the ring leader or the aggressor in the situation, making sure they're not called weak or scared.

People should care more about happiness instead of their image. Just think about every time you have an issue or problem. How do things work out when you respond with emotions in the midst of it? For me, it has always ended with another problem because I was responding from emotion instead of logic. In doing so, it only put a band-aid on the problem at hand. This was learned behavior from my parents because they never dealt with any of the issues that came up. Just like time keeps moving, so did the problems that came up. Even if my parents dealt with the problem at that moment, once that moment was over, then the problem was over. When I was a kid and would get in trouble, my punishments would never last long. When I was arrested at 16 years old for selling drugs, my parents were so mad at me. My dad was super disappointed, and I was mad at myself for disappointing him. My mom knew I sold drugs. She wasn't cool with it, but I was able to be more honest with my mom because she was more lenient than my dad.

It's always like that where one parent is cooler than the other. I think my mom was more cool because she liked to party and break rules. My dad has always been about business. This was another learned lesson. At a young age, I learned that I could get away with certain things with my mom and not my dad. I used that to my advantage to get what I wanted when I was in trouble and when I wanted something. As a consequence of getting arrested, my dad had put me on punishment for the whole summer, but of course, that didn't last. First off, he bought me a computer. Why would he buy me a computer while I was on punishment? I had begged him for it. Looking back, I know my parents were doing the best they knew how. My mom didn't really grow up with anything, and neither did my dad, so they tried to provide us with more than what they had. Even in the midst of it, my daddy was still trying to provide me with an opportunity to do right, to better myself, but I wasn't in a good place mentally to see that. In my mind, I was a spoiled brat, getting my way, who had parents that let me get away with everything. The reality was, they didn't know everything I was doing, and they believed in me. They didn't know that I had developed a lot of the things they'd shown me.

My parents saw good in me and all the while, I was doing bad. I'm so thankful for God's grace and mercy. He has shown me a way that has brought me to places that I thought were only in my imagination. He has blessed me to enjoy my peace. To enjoy not being in the midst of things anymore, but doing what makes me happy. I had to find my peace and get comfortable with me, as much as I would like to think that I had it all together. Had someone asked, I would have assured them that I loved me more than anything or anybody. That was not true, and I would have never known that it wasn't true until I went through my story. Seeing how every time I was in the midst of things the outcome was never good, I had to find real value in myself and when I did, life began to have meaning and purpose.

We are just halfway through the Power of Purpose. I hope that you're beginning to have a better understanding of situations when you're not taking it personally and finding the purpose will always have a better outcome and give you peace of mind. Now, when I'm in the midst of a situation that can disrupt my peace, I go to my wife about it. This gives me a different perspective on the situation. If it's a problem where she and I are not seeing eye to eye, I find a quiet place to listen to my private thoughts and pray to the Lord. Listening to my private thoughts allows me to go back and forth with myself, analyzing what's happening. This way, I control my emotions and keep from reacting. This allows me to keep my power, keeping all my energy instead of transferring my energy to her or vice versa. Self-control gives you power over all situations.

The next time you're quick to react in the midst of a bad, confusing, unsettling situation, take the time to stop, slow, think, open your mind and process how to proceed moving forward. This will help your situation end in peace instead of chaos. Don't worry about what people will think about you for not reacting, just remember that your life is meaningful, and you have a purpose to fulfill. Running around mad, angry, frustrated, and reacting to every little thing will keep you from accomplishing your dreams and goals. Don't get caught up in the midst of it; the battle has already been won. Pray about it, be patient, and let God be God.

Poem:

Why are things unclear?

Why is my mind so heavy?

I want to drive something besides a Chevy

The load gets light through the night

I pray to God He makes things right

Every door I walk in they tell me "No"

Then they reply, "thank you for coming and close the door"

I leave out feeling worse than I did before

In my mind, I'm screaming "Go"

Going through the process brings on fear

I'm taking back my power, listening to God's whisper in my ear

I'm learning my "Why," and things are now clear

By: Monique Turner

Chapter 5
Discovering Your Gifts

When you get to a point in your life that you begin to discover your gifts, talents and purpose from God, it will begin to change your life in ways that you probably thought were unreal. I remember being in grade school; I would always take extra dittos and books home, so we could play school on the weekends. I was always the teacher; I was so creative as a kid. I set up different classrooms, and the different levels of stairs were the different levels of grades. I would even organize picnics for us outside in the middle of the grass, so we didn't have to go to the park. Our projects had five courts. I lived in the first court, and every court was the same except the basketball court. All the courts were surrounded by red bricks that you could sit on and in the middle was grass and a tree. We didn't have to go to the park for grass; we had it right in front of us.

We did so many creative things as kids. We played all kinds of games, and in every game, I had to be the captain or first. In grade school, the teachers always said that I talked too much on my report cards. Who would have ever thought that talking was my gift from God? When I was younger, I would tell people that I wanted to be a lawyer. They would tell me that I would be a great lawyer because I love to argue. I don't know why arguing was my thing; I loved to be right and get the last word in. I know this is a habit that was developed from my dad. When I was a kid, my uncle Joe would call me "I Know" because every time they would say something, I would reply with "I Know." When I was in middle school, I was very free-spirited. I didn't feel like I had to hang with the in-crowd; I didn't have to hang with the people from my block; I hung with all the crowds, and I had a variety of friends. I would hang with the Asian kids and play Chinese kickball, the Hispanic kids and play soccer, and mixed kids to play softball. I'm glad that even though I was doing more than what I was seeing being done in my environment, I felt that I was still staying true to part of Monique.

It's crazy that I can look back and really say that when I was in middle school, I was selling drugs. I was doing what some adults were doing; I was doing what most adults were scared to do, and nobody knew it. I took photos in middle school; I would go to school an hour early to be in photo club. I was the only black kid, which didn't matter, as I was learning something new, and I enjoyed doing things outside my normal. When I was a little girl, I loved to help and feel like I was doing something meaningful. We would get free lunch and snack in the summertime in our projects. I would help the lunch instructor pass out lunches to the kids in our neighborhood, and she would give me a dollar, but I didn't do it for that.

Looking back, I can see now how everything was shaping me for everything that I'm doing now. We even had a guy who came to take us on field trips for the summer; it was like we had our own club for teens in the projects. The funny thing about that is, I would always tell him what we should be doing and how we should be doing it. I always had to run the show. My passion for kids started young, but it took me until 2010 after federal prison and serving my first federal probation violation to realize this. Discovering your gifts aren't easy. I was about to lose everything and then came the vision, but just because I had a vision doesn't mean that it was going to happen.

While I was serving my six-month probation violation, I was juggling a lot. I had to find time to get to my kids, who were in

Pittsburg, and I was living in San Francisco at the halfway house. God works it all out, even when you're not focused on Him, and He blessed me with a job at the Olive Garden in Pittsburg right on time. I had just got hired about two weeks before I had to start the violation. I don't even know what made me apply for them. I was with Gboo, and I told him to pull over so I could go get an application. The host in the front told me they were hiring, so I called the manager once this case came up and just like that, I was hired. This was perfect because I would work weekdays at the Olive Garden, and even though my kids didn't see me in the morning for school, they saw me after school and we would all sit down for dinner together. They thought I had to work another job. I know it was wrong to lie to my kids, but I couldn't disappoint them, especially my oldest son, who I had already put through so much. On weekends, I would work at Golden Eagle where we sold our chicken wings, and on Sundays, I did workshops at the YGC in Oakland. Once again, God was being him and setting it all up for me.

During this time, my cousin Bean had passed away from cancer. She was like a big sister to me; she was so awesome. She believed in me and left me $10,000 when she passed away to get myself started on my business. This was so sweet of her. At her repass, I started talking to her brother Vince, and I told him what I wanted to do, and he gave me the number of a guy named DB. He said that DB works at the YGC where he used to work and that he would hook me up; they run workshops up there with the youth on weekends. I gave him a call. At the time, the main reason was for me to get out the halfway house longer than the four hours that they gave me for a church pass. When I met DB, he was so cool, real and helpful. He let me come every weekend, using my plays that I had written to run the workshops. I was so excited, and the teens loved the plays. They felt that they could relate to the story.

Once I was released from the halfway house, I stopped going every weekend like I'd done before, but DB was always on my mind, so I called him to see if I could come and get some advice from him. I was trying to do workshops, and I didn't think I had the time management down like I should. So, DB let me come back and work on my material with the teens. I know that if it weren't for Bean passing away, I would never have met my mentor, and without him, I wouldn't have been in a position of knowing how to narrow things down. I would still be all over the place, thinking I could have an organization that serves all students from 5-18 years old, and that wasn't possible for me at that moment. I had to find my starting point, and because of my mentor, I did just that.

Here I was with a vision that I knew was my purpose, but everybody was doubting me. Everybody was telling me how it was not possible because I didn't have money or a college degree. I was on federal probation and now fighting a state case. In the beginning, I didn't listen to them, and I still tried to do everything I could to get this started. I called my good friend, "E," who'd been a friend for over 20 years. She was always there for me when I needed her. She was my smart friend, the friend out of my normal, who had graduated from UC Berkeley. I met "E" 20 years ago when we were both visiting our boyfriends in jail. For me, it was my son's father. We had grown a genuine relationship that we still share today. I called her and asked her if she could help me with my proposal for the organization. Like always, she agreed and sent me over a proposal.

Since I didn't have any money, I went to this law firm in San Francisco that helps people like me with no money work on their 501.C3. This is the paperwork that must be submitted to be considered a nonprofit. This was easy as I was in the halfway house that was also in San Francisco, but it was a very slow process since they were doing it for free. In the meantime, I decided to go to my old projects, Valencia Gardens, and talk with the manager to see if I could come in and run a program. I wanted this so badly! I wanted to run a program where I was raised and help the kids in the same community. The problem with that is that our plans don't always line up with God's plans. The answer was "No" because I didn't have a 501.C3, so they told me that I needed to get a fiscal sponsor. This is an organization that will sponsor you until you become eligible for your own 501.C3. I went around to different organizations trying to get someone to be my fiscal sponsor, and everyone kept telling me, "No." This was getting frustrating, and now I'm out of the halfway house, so, of course, my focus isn't the organization as much as it was.

I had to get back to work and making money. I had a family to take care of; my wife was working, and I also needed to be work-ing. At this time, it's the middle of 2010, and soon as I got out of the halfway house, I went back to breaking the law. This time, I had to do things on my own, as I couldn't risk being told on again. I was fighting the state case because two people had decided to tell on me while trying to save themselves. I told you about my friend who was getting the numbers for me, and then there was the girl who was using the sliders for me. When the police approached her, she told them everything. I couldn't believe this because I had done everything to try and keep her out of it, but they found her through her social media profile. Of course, she never told me that she'd told, but she didn't have to because the paperwork did all the telling.

It's important to know, don't do the crime if you can't do the time because snitching on someone to save yourself will never end well. It might save you for the moment, but in the long run, it will create more problems for you and give you the worst label you could have in the streets, and that's a "Snitch." My kids were playing basketball with the Junior Warriors, and I hooked up with the director and became his co-director. I was doing what I loved to do, working with kids, coaching basketball, so now I was coaching my kids and other kids in the community. God was once again showing me my gifts and talents. Even though I wasn't being paid, it felt so good, and I felt complete working with the youth. God was saving me once again, even though I wasn't being obedient to His calling for my life.

Let me show you about God's favor and how He will continue to show you He's God with you seeking him or not. The case that I was able to do house arrest for was out of Redwood City and since they were offering me nine months, they said that I could do it in their work furlough program, to avoid having to do it in the county jail. This would allow me to be in their live-in program for the nine months. They did an assessment and said, "No," they wouldn't take me, which was heartbreaking. I was so sad because this meant that I had to leave my family, and my kids would have to come to see me in jail. At this time, my relationship with God was growing, and I was attending church, sometimes on my own.

Once again, my good friend, "E" had told me about this church in Pittsburg called New Birth, so I decided to check it out; it was a nice big church. As before, I would sit in the back when I went, and every time I would find myself crying or sad because I felt that the bishop was always talking to me. My wife and kids didn't go to church with me; I would go when I felt that God was telling me to go. I've realized that when I got the vision, that was God showing himself to me; He was trusting me, my faith had grown in him, and even though I wasn't living right, I would call on him for everything. I now had a relationship with him, so after they told me 'No,' and my lawyer said there wasn't anything else we could do, I was crushed. All I could think about was the message that the Bishop had talked about when Jacob used the stone as a pillow, and when he woke up, he knew that God was there. (Genesis 28:11) I went to sleep with this on my mind, and just as God came to Jacob in his sleep, he came to me and gave me another vision. He told me to go to the halfway house that I was just discharged from a few months prior and see if they would accept me there. I was so excited when I woke up; I couldn't believe it. I told my wife that I knew that this was going to work out before I'd even gone to the halfway house.

I went to Geo halfway house and talked to the supervisor, and she and I were cool. I used to help wax the floors at night. I enjoyed doing this. I would do it with this guy named Bud, who was like my guardian Angel from God. I would always bring him clothes and food, and I was sad when I heard he'd gone back to prison. Because of him, I had built a great relationship with the staff. Before he got there, I couldn't stand the staff. I didn't like the way they talked to me or thought they were in control of my movement. The truth is, they were, and it was my fault for putting myself in those situations. I'm glad my daddy taught me to be good to people, not because of what they can do for you but because that's what God wants us to do. You never know who God will use to change your life or your circumstances. It's always the person you least expect because I would have thought that he would be the reason that made my next situation work out better than the one I'm in now.

I was talking to Maria, the supervisor, and I explained the situation to her. I then asked could I do my nine months through her program, and she said 'Yes.' Immediately, I called my attorney and told her the good news. She told me to have Maria write a letter saying that she was willing to accept me. We went back to court, and the judge agreed and allowed me to serve my nine months in the San Francisco halfway house. When I went to report to the halfway house, I thought I was reporting to turn myself in to live there for the next nine months. When I got there, I went to talk to my case manager, who then had me hooked up with an ankle monitor. This was so amazing; I was going home! I had to hurry and call my wife as she had left, thinking I had to stay there. This was unreal! How did I go from not being accepted in the only out of custody program that Redwood City offered to be accepted in another county and now getting house arrest instead of being in the halfway house?

I knew that God was shaking things up, and the Lord had given me freedom. My probation officer at the time couldn't believe it; she said she had never seen anything like this before, I told her, this is all God's doing, and when He's involved, He performs miracles. I was overjoyed that once again, I would be able to do this without my kids knowing, which was my biggest concern. My issue with that now is if they were my biggest concern, then I should have given up the street life, but nope, I wasn't ready to let go of the street image, plus all my friends were from the streets. I kept telling myself that everything I was doing was for them, but I can see now how that was only partly true. I was doing it to feel good, earn money, feel empowered, and not feel worthless to my wife. The enemy was controlling my mind, and every time I would get one step closer with God, he would try to pull me five steps closer to him. I had to learn to care less about what I could see and more about what I envisioned. I knew faith without works was dead, so it was time to start letting my faith live again.

While I was on the ankle monitor, I started doing the workshops at the YGC. Of course, this way, I get more time out. See, I knew how to work the system as the system was trying to work me. My monitor didn't have GPS tracking, so I could be wherever I wanted to be. Things were going good; I was doing the groups, had a job, volunteering at the boys and girls club. Things seemed to be moving and moving with a purpose. When God gave me house arrest instead of the halfway house again or jail, it blew my mind. He kept showing me that my life had purpose and meaning and even though my faith in him was growing every day, I was starting to realize that I needed to make some changes in my life, but that wasn't going to happen overnight. The funny thing is when I would do wrong now, it would eat at my conscience, and this became annoying to me. The more I did wrong, the more I knew I needed to do right.

Finally, I got off house arrest and was able to do what I wanted to do. I was tired of working at the Olive Garden; I was tired of serving people that would leave me no tip or a few dollars. I knew this was God, I knew that this job was a part of my test. He was testing how I would serve others; while at the Olive Garden, He was also using me for his purpose. I had a co-worker, who was fighting a custody battle to see his kids, and while he was telling me the story, God was telling me to pray with him. Now, this was weird! I had never asked someone if we could pray together. We went into the back room where it was just us; we joined hands, and I prayed with him. Next week after his court date, he was so happy at work and gave me a big hug because he'd won and had been granted visitation with his kids. This was so exciting to see God using me for his purpose. I would never have prayed with someone in the past.

My life was making a shift without me even knowing it. I wasn't doing anything to force myself to change; God was guiding me, and I was being obedient to his call. God was showing me my gifts, but at this time, I didn't see it; I just knew that he was using me. It didn't matter who, what, where, when, or why. If someone needed to vent, then I was right there to listen and give them advice. When I was working at the coffee company, Jerimiah's, I did meet lots of people on my route. I would pray with my co-workers when they were having issues, and I was always giving advice as if I was a relationship expert. Even when I would make my deliveries, the workers in the stores would talk to me about their problems. I remember this lady told me that I have a good spirit; that's been told to me a bunch of times. When your spirit is good, everything else will line up good in your life.

My life was perfect to me growing up as a kid, teenager, young adult and adult, despite all my wrongdoings and run-ins with the law, lack of parenting, and being selfish most of my life this far. I'm so thankful that God showed me my gifts and many talents; his blessings inspired me to be a better me every day. I'm honored that He believed in me when I didn't believe in myself. He has humbled me and taught me that none of this is for me or about me. It's all for his purpose. I know now that if I didn't go through the different life challenges that I had to endure, I never would have discovered my gifts.

When I was in prison, I would talk with a lot of women and give them advice on the different things they were struggling with. I had no idea that speaking would turn out to be my gift from God. I know that everyone used to always tell me that I talked too much, but that didn't mean anything, so I thought. If my friend had never come into my room while I was crying my heart out about my father, I don't know if I would have this strong relationship with God today. See, God uses people for his purpose in our time of happiness and despair. It was my daddy's birthday, and every year on his birthday, I would lose my mind. I was dealing with a lot of guilt from losing my dad. I felt that I should have spent more time with him since I knew he was dying. I barely went down to their house. I wasn't strong enough. The most important man in my life was dying, and I didn't know how to deal with my dad looking like that. I didn't understand how the doctors could give him six months to live. The thought of him having cancer and dying made me weak, and when he passed away, I beat myself up about it every day for seven years. The terrible thing about this is that I was in prison for four of those seven years.

While I was on the streets, I had my family and friends to occupy my time alone with substance abuse, drugs and alcohol. In prison, I didn't have anybody. I had friends, I even had a girlfriend, but none of that mattered. All that mattered at that moment was that I didn't have my daddy, and I never would see him in the flesh again, and that was all I could think about. I was being selfish to my own feelings because the way my daddy was looking, I know he's in a better place. He was suffering, and now he's watching over me. So, once I started bible studies with my friend, and I started to see God, things began to shift for me.

Let me tell you about the first time I saw God answer my prayer. My roommate had been calling her daughter for years. She used to speak to her, but the father stopped answering the phone when she would call. Now that I've been having bible study with my friend, I started to pray for my roommate to speak with her daughter and sure enough, about three months later, she came into the room so happy. She was screaming with joy that she'd talked to her daughter. That was the beginning of a wonderful relationship with God and I. I remember a few months after I lost my mom, it was a Sunday, and I was so sad. I was missing my parents and really felt like I needed God, so he led me to the church up the street from the house. It was a really small church, and I had been here before with my sister on Easter or Mother's Day in the past. I was so skeptical. Should I go or not because I had on a Roca Wear sweatsuit and Timberland boots?

But the spirit led me in. I tried to sit in the back because I was uncomfortable, and then one of God's angels brought me to the front with her. I felt so welcomed and loved; I felt God; I felt my parents. I didn't pay attention then, how moments like that were me hearing from God and letting him lead me. There have been so many situations where God has called on me, and when I'm obedient to him and his word, everything always works out. At that moment, I needed comfort, and God gave me comfort through his people. I was grieving; I was a lost soul, and I praise God that He didn't let me wander deeper into the wilderness.

Do you know that my gift to write was discovered when I was in the 11th grade? My teacher told me to write a poem. I wrote about a whale, and she thought it was so amazing. Telling stories has been my thing since I was a teen and probably before that as nobody helped bring that side of me out. At John O'Connell, I enrolled in advertising. I really enjoyed making commercials, and now I really enjoy writing plays and scripts. After the 11th grade at John O'Connell, I went back to Mission High, so it was back to the hood of things. Mission was five blocks from home, and John O'Connell was all the way in the Avenues, so it was a different crowd of kids. Our gifts don't just come out the blue, our gifts are living inside of us, and being sharpened since the day we are born.

Our gifts are shown in all different areas of our life. In tapping into your true authentic self, you have to relive your past because the things you've been so passionate about all your life is aligned with your gift. The more I write this book and reflect on my childhood, the more I realize that I'm setting myself free from all the past trauma I've experienced. My gift is speaking. I have a couple that keeps fighting. They have a 4-year-old son together, the father was in and out of jail, and now they can't seem to have a solid relationship. Every time they fight, the baby is right there in the middle. I have given them safe words and boundaries; the problem with that is none of this is working because there's a lot of underlying issues that need to be relived before they can work through the things happening on the surface.

I know that God wants me to help them overcome these issues, either together or apart, and this is an area that I know all so well. A lot of the issues that they're dealing with are the same issues that me and my son's father went through when our son was three years old. The father has issues from his childhood, not being loved the way he feels he should have been loved, and because of this, he's looking for that love from his son's mother. They have been together since he was 15, and she was 18. He has been in and out of jail and lived a street life. He's now trying to do better for himself and his family. The problem with that is he needs to be serious about doing better for himself before he can be the man he needs to be for them. He needs to let go of the burdens that he's living with from his childhood and focus on making his son's childhood better than his parents made his. He's only 20 years old, so even though he talks about doing right by his son, he's always doing the opposite when things get tough with him and his baby's mama. You can't expect to make any relationship work if you don't have a clue who you are, what you like, and what you want out of life. Wasting time on dead relationships can delay your journey of discovering your gifts. When I'm helping people and troubleshooting solutions to their problems, I always stay neutral for both parties involved, helping them see that it's never personal, but it's always a purpose, even in the midst of the chaos.

POEM:

It's easy to have a million things on your mind

There comes a time when you need to leave people behind

Your ladder isn't for everyone to climb

The clutter seems to overtake my mind

I remain humble with my eyes on the prize

Thankful God keeps me on the rise

I'm in the driver seat of this car ride

God is my Google; I'm grateful for my personal tour guide

With him, I don't have to tell no lie

God, you give me tears of joy in my eyes

God, thank you for covering my family and surrounding the blue sky

By: Monique Turner

Chapter 6
New Opportunities

When you discover your gifts, talents and purpose, old doors will close, and new doors will open. When I first discovered my purpose, I worked on trying to bring it to pass. The problem with that is my mind was still in the gutter. I had to live and provide for my family, not to mention the fact that I didn't have any money to purchase everything we needed in order to get the business started. Here it was, December 2010, and the vision is clear. Still, everyone is doubting me, and I don't have the education, money, resources, or connections that I need to get the ball rolling. Initially, this isn't how I was thinking, but I was allowing everyone else to give me a negative, pessimistic mindset. They were focused on their perception of me, and I almost fell into the trap because I was getting a few Nos here and there. Walking into purpose isn't easy and sometimes, the path, people and connections are looking right at you, but if you're not mentally aware, then you can miss it all.

Even though many people were doubting me, I didn't let that stop me. I let it motivate me to want more and never settle. I love the number three, and I believe there is power in that number. Jesus rose on the third day, and I believe that everything comes in threes. From 2010 - 2013, I was a mess. I was battling with loving myself, feeling loved, finding my purpose, trusting my visions, trusting my faith, and surrendering my life to God. This ride felt neverending and had me questioning myself all the time. "Is this right? Can I do this? Will God forgive me for this? Will I lose everything? Can I stop doing this? When will I catch a break? Why is everyone saying 'No'? and when will I get a contract? Finally, in the winter of 2013, I got a call from my oldest son's high school. They were calling about his absence and tardies. This made me furious because I didn't understand why they weren't calling about the 'Ds and 'Fs that he was getting. They didn't care about that; they cared about missing their money when he wasn't sitting in that seat. That's a huge problem in our school systems today.

Parents, advocate for your child, make sure they're getting all the resources they need in order to be successful in their current grade and moving forward. When you see your child's grades declining, check into it. Don't just put punish your child for bad grades, go to the school and meet with the teacher. Get a better understanding of why his/her grades are like this. Every child learns differently, yet every teacher is teaching every child the same. This is something I had to realize. I had one son who didn't care to learn how they were teaching and another son, who was okay with their teaching method. I had a meeting set up with the Dean, who began telling me about a program they had on their campus for young men and wanted my permission to sign my son up. I told them it should be mandatory for students that were failing like my son, and they agreed. I later discussed my belief with them that the school needed teachers that paid better attention to all their students. To hear a teacher tell me that my son was a good kid who had fallen through the cracks had me furious.

I started telling them about my program that I was running at the YGC, and they were intrigued by what I was saying and what I had to show them. Even though I was going to my son's school to speak about my son's grades and options moving forward, I went with a mission. I knew this was God possibly giving me an opportunity, so I had my materials with me. I wanted more information on how programs worked their way into the schools. Even though I had learned how to do workshops with youth, I was clueless about how to run a workshop at a school or what to do with the youth. This was the fear in me. This was me doubting myself. This was me letting all those negative people into my consciousness.

After speaking with the Dean, he told the Principal that he needed to speak with me, and he came into our meeting. I discussed what I felt to be a good program. He immediately asked me when I could start. I told him tomorrow! I informed them both that I didn't have a business license, my 501.C3, or anything. All I had was a vision and the plays I had written for the YGC workshops. I started volunteering in January 2013 and was given a caseload of 14 girls. Everything was great, just like when I was in school. I was speechless, overjoyed with happiness, and then God tested my faith once again. He needed to see what I would do under pressure.

When I started working at the school, I gave up illegal hustling. I was scared of God taking what He had given me. He had given it to me without me having to change who I was or compromise myself. All I had to do was be where He wanted me to be. This was a dream come true. The man that was running the program for young men was super cool. He helped me with what I needed to do in order to start my business. All I had to do was everything I had already done for the previous businesses that we started. See, even though the other businesses didn't work out, it was the setup for what was to come. It was a miracle. All the questions I had were being answered, and all the doubt I was feeling had been replaced with possibilities. God will send you to the right place at the right time and provide you with the right people to see each mission through. I was on top of the world. This was the best feeling ever, and even though I was only volunteering, I was on cloud nine. After three years of hearing "No," I finally get a "Yes" out of the blue. It was so unexpected, but again, God's spirit told me to bring evidence of my passion with me, and I was ready. I wasn't sure how my son was going to react, knowing that I was going to be working at his school, but he was excited. As I told you earlier, I wanted to do the nonprofit in my neighborhood in San Francisco, but this wasn't God's plan.

Pittsburg is where it all began. The opportunities we get are not always what we might expect them to be because it's not about what we want to do; it's about God's plan, and when we're obedient, doors open that you thought would stay closed, and opportunities come when you least expect. God turned those "Nos" into "New Opportunities." Everything that I'd been through trying to get this started came to fruition because of a call from my son's high school about his absences. What's even more crazy is the call came at 7 pm. Normally, I wouldn't even answer the phone when it was the school number because it's always a recorded message. Now, you all know I have a criminal record, so once I did my fingerprints, they came back, and it wasn't good. The difference between this time and the last time was that I told the Principal about my record when he wanted to hire me. I was very honest with him about my past, so when everything came up, it wasn't a surprise.

I'm glad that my faith in God was stronger than it was seven years ago because if it weren't, then they would've pulled me from the school that same day. I wanted that stationary engineering position so badly because of the pay. I also liked the things that I was learning, but for the most part, it was about the money. Losing that job was heartbreaking at that moment but looking back, it was the setup that I needed. See, God knew that the enemy had my mind. He knew that I was still lost. Even though I did five years in prison, I still didn't change, but he didn't give up on me. He allowed me to see the burning bush, as He did Moses, and now it was time to put his plan into action. I'm glad that I started to trust God instead of only trusting myself. And as always, here comes God with another test of faith.

I was doing a good job with my students; my record came back, and all of my arrests showed up; it even mentioned my federal and state probation. I just knew this was going to be it. I was so mad when I got the call that the Principal wanted me to come in the next day so that we could talk. I was so nervous, but I had faith that God had a plan. I knew He didn't let me in this school to put me out. I had given up everything, and I felt as though I was finally living right for the first time in my life. I was doing things according to God's plan instead of my own. The next morning, I went to see the Principal as he requested. He told me that he liked the work that I was doing with the girls, and he was pushing for me to stay. He'd spoken with the superintendent, and they agreed that I could stay under the condition that I wouldn't be alone with the students. I had to conduct my groups in the library, a common area with the girls. I was so happy.

All I could think about was how amazing God was. He was really directing my path and bringing my vision to life. He was doing all this for his purpose for my life and not because I was living a life without sin or going to church every Sunday. The crazy thing is, this blessing came at a time when I had lost my focus on the nonprofit. When this was all happening, I was working, making good money again as a cement mason. It was wintertime, and during the winter, we barely worked because of the rain. This gave me the space I needed to pursue the nonprofit without a second thought. A few people knew about my past record; some judged me, not to my face but, of course, chatter can be worse than being approached with the truth. The hood in me used to want to flash, but then my daddy would always come to me through the spirit, reminding me to treat people good, and God will treat you good. My daddy told me that when I was running around, being a hard-headed teenager. I didn't pay attention then, but I know exactly what he was teaching me now. So, I didn't let the chatter bother me. They were mad, and I was happy, actually overjoyed, so I didn't let their issue with my success become my issue. I even knew the ones that were chattering. I would make it a point to speak to them. Their response would be mad sometimes, and I would laugh to myself. The funny thing is, the same people that were rooting for me to get a contract in the beginning knew about my record and now they're the same ones who are talking behind my back.

The enemy will use who and what he can to get you off your path. See, when God shows up, the enemy shows up. Your faith in God has to be grounded in all situations. You have to know everything is according to his plan, the good and the bad. The most important thing to do is always pray and ask God to direct your path all the days of your life. Believe that God is more powerful. He is the almighty; He died for our sins, and failing isn't an option. Every day, you have a chance at a new opportunity. You can either dwell on the past, or you can keep pursuing your future. The devil is a lie. Just because things go wrong doesn't mean they won't go right. God doesn't give us anything that we can't handle, and when you have faith in that and believe in that, you should never give up. I almost gave up on my opportunity to be the founder of a nonprofit, to serve God's children, and then here came God showing me He has the final say; He is the king. Everything that I thought was wrong or bad in my life, God has allowed me to see it as good and use it to help heal others. Believe in your journey and keep God first.

It was the end of the school year, and I did great; they're ready to give me a $10,000 contract for one day a week. This was so awesome. I had given up my job as a cement mason making $44hr. No amount of money is worth waking up early doing what makes you unhappy. I lived all my life worried about money. It's crazy when I think about it. I started hustling at 10 years old, and at 35, I was turning over a new leaf. I was walking by faith and not by sight. I was trusting the process. I prepared all my paperwork to present to the board and was awarded the contract for the upcoming school year. Now that it's summertime, I wanted to do a summer program because I knew that the city didn't have anything for the youth to do during summertime. I went to everyone in the city, the district office, other organizations, the city office and the school board trying to see if I could get a summer location. Here we go once again with the "No." I was really allowing this to frustrate me for a minute, and then I took my focus off me and began to petition God for what he wanted me to do through prayer, asking that He show me his way.

Of course, with God on my side, it's all possible, and just like that, the city of Pittsburg allowed us to use their conference office to run our groups in the summer. We had fun in the summer. We worked on the play, did tie-dyed socks, and took fun field trips. All this was out of pocket. I hadn't made any money since I started doing this, but I had invested so much. One day while at the summer program, I got a call from someone asking me about doing their credit card numbers. This was illegal, and I had given up doing illegal activity for six months now. I wanted to respond with "Yes," but in my mind, I knew that this was the enemy trying to tempt me. He knew I was vulnerable and in need of money. Once again, we had a rental car that needed to go back, and if that happened, then I wouldn't have transportation to get the girls to and from the summer program.

My back was against the wall, but my fear for God was stronger than my need for money. I told her "No," I couldn't do it, and a few minutes later, I got a call from Gboo, telling me about a car dealership in Modesto. I told my wife when she came home that we needed to go check it out, as we couldn't continue to afford a rental car; we needed another car. God is so amazing. We went to the dealership and left the lot with a brand new car without putting $1 down. This had never happened to us before; we had to put $5,000 down when we got the truck, and it was used. I knew it was all God, but looking back, I don't know how we were surviving with me not working and my wife supporting us financially. It was the power of God. It's all about the unseen and having faith.

Because of our faith in God; He continued to give us a new opportunity. The district office was giving away their yearly grant, the Keller Canyon Grant. I didn't have my 501C.3 at the time, so I couldn't apply on my own, so I needed a fiscal sponsor. The supervisor of our district sent me to Rivertown to speak with the Executive Director about being my fiscal sponsor. With only two months left, God's blessings came once again for the direction to go to Rivertown and meet with their staff. I met Susie, and she was the best. She agreed to write the grant for me. She was a blessing from God. She didn't want any money; all she wanted was to be paid in chocolate. This couldn't have been a better arrangement since I didn't have any money to offer. She wrote the grant, and we were awarded $2,500. I was so excited. I just knew this was the beginning to something so great.

Susie later connected me with a lady named Karen. She was another angel sent from God. I didn't have money to pay her to do the paperwork for our 501.C3, but she was willing to work with me. She said she would accept payments, so I gave her $100 every month. Money was so tight, and I'm so grateful she understood my situation. Again, this was all God. She got everything done in about six months. She informed me that I needed to get a $1,000 to send the paperwork off. We had just got our taxes back, so we used some of that money to pay for the paperwork. God was lining everything up and making way for us to see this through. I couldn't believe it! I was so amazed; it was unreal.

God was blessing us with our own nonprofit. He put the right people in the right place at the right time. All I had to do was follow my spirit and be obedient to every word. God was making the unbelievable happen with the one that they counted out, criticized, and judged. Watching God perform all these different miracles right before my eyes gave me the determination to seek him more, call on him and lean on him for all things. I never had to question, Is there a God? I was watching him do what no man could do. I was watching him make me powerful in areas that I was weak. When you're a living witness to God's great works, don't keep that quiet. Speak about it, read about it, and pray about it. He is the almighty that lives inside all of us.

A new school year had started, and my girls are in the 10th grade. Since I'm on a contract, they are giving me more girls, and the administration is seeing my success in helping them solve problems and deal with their social-emotional issues. It's December 2013, and the Principal let me know that there's been so much talk amongst the administration about me being on probation, and there is nothing he can do. I would have to get everything cleared, or I would lose my contract. I had until the following semester, which was January 2014, a few weeks away. I went to the courts, and they told me that there was nothing they could do and that it would take six to eight weeks before I would be able to get on the calendar. I spoke with a lawyer, who informed me that I could do the work myself. All I needed to do was go to the law library, write up a motion, and submit it to the courts. I did just that. My cousin Smoothie and I went to the law library, submitted the paperwork, and received a court date two weeks out. This was perfect. I had a letter from the Principal, stating that I was doing a great job with the students. I addressed how I'd found my purpose and told the judge that without this opportunity, I would lose it all. The judge released me from probation. This was so exciting; I couldn't believe it! This wasn't something that happens every day. God was really blessing me. I knew it wasn't about me; it was about the gift He gave me and the purpose He intended for me to bless others.

The next step was to get my record expunged. This way, nobody would be able to bring up my past again. Smoothie and I did the paperwork once again, submitted it, and had a court date in another two weeks. We had never done this before, and any other time, we would have accepted what was given to us and settled for them telling me it would take six to eight weeks, but when God is involved, it's all about trusting the process. I'm so thankful for the journey I was on, trusting God and everything that I envisioned. When we finally got back in court for the expungement, I was so nervous, but I know that God didn't bring me this far to take it from me. I was doing everything right, or so I thought. I still owed $1,500 in restitution. This could have been a deal-breaker, but once again, God let it be known that He was in control. My record was expunged, and the $1,500 restitution was released as well. I was so happy leaving the courthouse.

Words couldn't describe the joy I was feeling. I was amazed! God was playing favorites with me; He was showing me that it didn't matter who wanted me out or who counted me out. He counted me in, and He's in control of every outcome. He gave me the vision for Family Purpose, the name of our organization. It was funny because a year later, March 2015, the paperwork came in the mail, stating that we were officially a 501.C3 tax-exempt organization and what's more- they backdated it to 2013 when the paperwork was initially filed. I was so happy. I knew I had envisioned it, and I had faith that it would happen, but in the back of my mind, there was always that seed of doubt.

The name Family Purpose came from a vision as well. Originally, I thought the name of the nonprofit would be Successful Youth, but this name wasn't available. The representative from Go-Daddy, a domain registrar, kept searching names, and he kept offering us different variations since Successful Youth wasn't available, and finally, he suggested Successful Purpose. We all agreed this was it, except that was the name we were using for our visual arts program. So, being the visionary that I am, I saw the nonprofit being called Family Purpose. The team loved it, and it was available, so we decided to take it. God wanted every name to have purpose in it, literally and figuratively. This way, we don't lose sight of the mission at hand, which is to serve. When you're going through the process, it's important that you stay strong, not letting the enemy tempt you, listen to your conscious mind, don't settle, know your worth, and be true to yourself.

I didn't know if I was coming or going, but that was okay because God had me every step of the way. When you're trusting the process, this means you're not trusting your flesh. The flesh is everything and everyone that looks good. You don't want anything easy, or the old way. You don't want everything that looks good because everything that glitters ain't gold. When you witness that mustard seed of faith grow in you, you must not let anything break it. Activate it more. Pray. Ask the father to make your view clear. Ask him for forgiveness and ask him for all that your heart desires. I was asking God for everything, but most importantly, I was thanking him and petitioning him for each blessing He presented me with.

Even though I wanted a community center of my own for the nonprofit, I celebrated every day I witnessed any progress. I praised God that He blessed me to receive the many things I would vision or pray for. I went to the school district to give them my paperwork and then I went to the Principal to inform him of the good news. He was happy for me. It was back to business! My cousin, Smoothie, was helping me work on this nonprofit. My wife was also a big part of it, although she worked full time for PG&E. But she was my right hand, helping me edit all my plays, making hundreds of copies at her job. When we started this, it was just her and me for the first three years, then God sent us Smoothie, and it was on from there. Smoothie was everything I needed at the time. She helped take the stress off of my wife and me because I'm really bossy, pushy, and annoying at times. That's because when I get a vision, I want to run with it, and you have to be ready. My wife would be ready, but I wouldn't take into consideration the fact that she had already worked a full day and was coming home to another full-time job. So, with Smoothie, it was just her and me. She didn't have another job at the time, so she was 100% committed to Family Purpose.

God was working everything out. It was so wild how he kept giving me what I needed and who I needed at the right time. I would stress my wife out at times to the point that we felt like we couldn't work together. This was okay because I had always prayed that God blessed me with the ability to take care of my wife for the rest of her life. Her job paid her good money, and I'm grateful for that because that is what made it possible for me to give up my job and trust the process. My wife would commute all the way to the city. She would leave the house at 5 am to be at work at 7 am. When I used to ride with her, it was cool, but now I was working down the street at the high school. I was getting up at 7 am, the time she had to be at work. I didn't have to fight with traffic for hours to get home as she did. I kept praying for the day to come soon that my wife would be able to leave her job and work with us full-time. She took care of our family financially; she never threw it in my face, and she never complained. She's my MVP. After working at PG&E all day, she would come home and do a cooking class at the Senior Center with our girls. We were blessed with a location at No Charge to run a teen cooking program at the senior center.

We were a great team of three, but growth was on the horizon. In the middle of the year, I was approached by the VP, who asked me if I wanted to be a part of this other program that they were offering. This was great because my contract wasn't very much, so this opportunity gave me an extra income. Once again, God was blessing me, opening up doors, creating new opportunities, and connecting me with people that I would grow with beyond this program. I was working with a few teachers, and most importantly, I got hooked up with Ms. Jenkins. She used to be my oldest son's English teacher. She was the only teacher who cared about his education. We hit it off immediately. She started giving me a platform to pilot my many visions in her classroom. From there, our relationship grew, and today she's a big part of Family Purpose. She's now our Director of Education and so much more. I consider her a good friend. She believes in me, supports my visions, and helps keep me grounded when I'm all over the place.

Now I was on a mission to get more contracts. I needed this organization to grow. I needed to make more money so that I could do more with my students, and God was blessing me with opportunities to make that happen; of course, not as fast as I would like, but I had to trust the process. When I got everything ex-punged, we were in the middle of the school year, and summer was approaching again. This time, the Principal wanted me to be at the school for two to three days. I was excited to see how we were moving up. They were willing to give me a $20,000 contract for the additional days during the upcoming school year, and I was getting a summer school contract. This was exciting! I went to the board, and they voted me in again. We did the summer program again, and the great thing about this is we got a summer school contract to actually run a summer program at the school. The seeds we were planting were showing the harvest.

Now, my original 14 girls are juniors in high school, and my caseload has grown to over 50 students. Everything is working out. We have office space at Rivertown, and this is where Smoothie would work. We applied for Keller Canyon again but were denied. This didn't make any sense to me, especially considering how much we had grown since the last opportunity to apply for the grant. I didn't let that hold me back. We started the new year off stronger than before. The new contract afforded us the opportunity to have Smoothie with me at the school. This was good because it freed me up to do more things. The previous year, she spent most of her time at the office, but once she started to be with me at the school, we let the office go. I didn't want to because it felt like we were mov-ing backward, but that wasn't the case. We were actually growing. I had to learn that the office space didn't add value or lessen the worth of our organization. It's all about perception.

Given our new opportunities, I wanted to continue to see where God was leading me, so I got out there and went to a few middle schools in hopes of securing a contract so that we could de-velop a feeder pattern. This way, we would be able to reach the students in secondary school; the younger, the better. I had a meeting with the Hillview Principal. He loved me. He informed me that he didn't have any money but set up a meeting with me and the district's director of after school programs. She liked what I presented, and we were blessed with an after-school contract. This was so amazing! I couldn't believe it. Now I had to hire a few people, so I called a friend, and she agreed to work with us and Ms. Jenkins. I also used my students as peer-educators. This was a really good program. We would go to the middle school and run workshops with about 30 students per school site, it was three sites.

We continued this for two years, and then I had to let the contract go. I had an Executive decision to make, keep the contract, the easiest $40,000 that I would ever get, or let it go because it didn't 't line up with the value, mission, goals and integrity of our program. Here it was. We were doing so good. The struggle was over, but I just kept thinking, what would happen if I give up this contract? I remember when money was tight, one year the landlords came and gave us a three-day notice to pay or quit. Our PG&E was $1,500. Thank God for payment plans. Things were so bad when it came to finances, but things were so amazing when it came to my inner happiness, peace, and love. I was doing exactly what I loved. I'd found my calling, but trusting the process was hard, especially since I knew how to get some fast money. But then I would always reflect on how far God had brought me, and my faith in him wouldn't let me give up on him, myself, or our family.

I couldn't do anything to jeopardize my freedom. My auntie was living with us at the time, and she helped us out and gave us $500. We were able to get the other $1600 to pay the rent. I didn't ever want to go back to living like that, but I knew God put this on my heart, and this was a moment of him testing me. Was I in it for the money or the purpose? It was absolutely for the purpose, so I made the decision to stop doing the after-school program. It was disappointing to my high school students as they enjoyed going to the middle schools and working with the younger students on their homework and facilitating after school activities with them. I had to trust that giving it up would make it greater later. The contracts continued to grow each year. Having Smoothie with me really allowed me to make new things happen on another level. Giving up the after-school contract put a huge dent in my pocket for the moment, but I knew that was a test from God. Past experience has shown me that when he closes one door, he opens another.

I was blessed with another contract for the continuation High School in Pittsburg. The funny thing is I'd seen myself working at this school previously. I had a passion for this school because this is the school my son transferred to and graduated from with honors. All the teachers cared and had compassion for their students here. Smoothie went to start this school, which was so good. Who would have ever thought we would be in multiple schools? Everyone told me this was impossible. They doubted me for so many reasons, and God showed them and me that He is God, and He has the final say. If I didn't trust the process, I would've been back in the streets doing the opposite of what God wanted me to do. I would have been doing what I knew how to do. See, even though this was my passion, all of this was way out of my element. I didn't go to school for this, and neither did the people who were doing this with me. I kept asking myself, 'How am I going to run a nonprofit?' Every time, God would respond by sending me the right contact or having me in the right place at the right time. Now, we're in two schools, and our contract at Pittsburg High has grown to four days. My finances were growing, and so was our organization. This was the best feeling in the world.

My third year arrived, and I had contracts at two different schools. Pittsburg was having a drug problem, so I hired a drug counselor to come run groups with the students that were getting caught using or selling. I felt like I needed to start a drug program, so I was on a mission, setting up meetings with the right people from the county to talk about funding. I met the right person, and she gave me all the pointers I needed to try and see this through. I went to the city of Pittsburg, did the paperwork that was needed to start the business, and I even found the perfect location. This was exciting! All I needed was the planning department to approve it and finish all the paperwork with the county. Everything seemed to be going well, according to plan, the only problem was that this wasn't for me. It was a necessary program, but this wasn't a part of my long-term purpose. This was me providing a temporary fix, and I'm honored that God trusted me to fix it at that moment.

I received so much opposition from staff, who didn't want me to have anything to do with a drug program because they had been working on getting another program, which they believed was more established and reputable. I wasn't trying to step on anyone's toes; I was just trying to fix a problem. The Principal, on the other hand, was very supportive. I appreciate him so much for believing in me and trusting me with his students. Despite my past record, because the truth is he had the power to say I had to go. Instead, he kept me and supported everything I wanted to do with the students. I know our spirits are aligned, and we're on a mission for God. See, when God is the head of everything you do, you don't have to do anything except let him lead and trust the process along the way. I was doing a great job, really making a difference in helping the youth deal with their social-emotional issues. When I see a need for young people in the community, I try to fix it.

The Family Purpose staff list was increasing, my cousin

Smoothie, my wife Tiffany, who is running an after-school cooking program, and now I've brought in a drug counselor to help our students. I did this all because of the need and my passion. I didn't receive any additional funds to support the additional work and programming. Even though I was giving my all trying to be the superwoman of the school, so many people were feeling threatened and intimidated by my ambition to support the students. My drug program ran for the rest of the school year, 2015, but the school site council also agreed to bring on the 'more reputable' drug program. I went to the planning department, and somehow, there was a mix-up, and my paperwork got denied, which was so frustrating, and I felt like I had lost. The staff were getting what they wanted, and that was frustrating. I hated to feel like I'd lost. In reality, God wasn't giving me more than I could handle. I couldn't let my ego get in the way of God's plan.

It was getting close to the summer, and the time was coming to renew the contract. At this point, I believe we were ready for a five-day contract. This was super exciting. Though I felt like I had lost at that moment, the truth is, I was winning big time. God was showing me that I needed to stick to the things I was good at, and just because I've experienced drug use, a drug home, parents on drugs, and selling drugs doesn't mean I have to do a drug program. I needed to partner with other organizations. That would make me stronger and keep me from getting burnt out so fast. As you know, I can be all over the place. I think I can do it all. This gets me in trouble a lot, especially with my team. I drive them crazy sometimes with these visions of mine; the same way I used to drive my wife crazy when it was just me and her. She always jokes about that. A lot comes easy and right on time, but the test and lessons can sometimes come at a price that you don't want to pay, so be very careful how you proceed.

Even though this door was closing, it allowed me to help a different group of students that I would have never met. It also allowed our organization to make a shift. Instead of serving only African American young ladies, we were now in a position to serve everybody. This was great actually. But, you know how it goes. As soon as everything is going well, here comes the curveball. Staff members that were against me didn't want me working with the young men. So, instead of continuing to get in a battle with staff about my program, I learned to do what I knew was right in my heart, what I felt God was telling me to do. I wasn't backing down, I was here to serve, and that's what I was going to do. Here we were in our fourth year, full contract, serving five days at Pittsburg and three days at Black Diamond. Our data was and continues to be, amazing. We had the best out of all the other programs on campus. Our participants started our program at a 0.97 overall GPA, and by the end of their junior year, we're at 2.33 overall, with a 100% graduation rate. The students that I started with are now seniors, and most of them don't have a plan after high school. This was troubling to me. I felt that I had failed them. I should have had them prepared for the next level. Even though I did the job they hired me to do and more, that wasn't good enough for me.

Here came another vision. We needed to start a program that helps students with SAT prep, college applications, and more. My wife was really smart, so I asked her and Ms. Jenkins to work on a program that could be our College track program. They came up with our AAA program (Academics, Accountability, Advocacy). The first year this program didn't really do what it was supposed to do, but the seed was planted. We weren't receiving any funding for this program yet, and once again, this meant we were running a program because of the need for the students, not because we were being paid. My prayers were being answered. My wife's department closed in 2015. We knew this was coming, and we were ready. A lot of people kept asking her if she was scared and what she was going to do now. She would tell them she was going to run her nonprofit.

Even though I got the vision years ago, God was bringing it to pass when he felt we were ready. The year is going well. I'm not at the schools as much because I began working on the administrative side of things more and had the vision to begin writing a book. But because of all the work that had been done, this was possible, Smoothie, my wife, and Ms. Jenkins pretty much have the schools covered. Ms. Jenkins was a teacher, but she was always there if we needed help with something, plus we worked with the same kids. She's like a mentor/editor, not to mention my friend. Everything is going so well. I just know that we're going to get a great contract for the next school year. I was thinking that they would pay for two people at the school instead of just me, given all that I had provided for them daily. But here comes the opposition once again. Every time I think it's all good, then boom.

The Principal told me that our contract would be cut in half because of budget cuts and now they want us to do half days. This had me so mad. What were we going to do? My wife doesn't have her corporate job anymore. She received unemployment for six months, but then for whatever reason, it stopped. We were up shit creek once again! Summer was coming, and we had no income because school is out and on top of that, you're telling me our contract will be cut in half. I had two options: figure something out or sit around talking about it. Here came the visions again. God gave me the vision to put together a packet and drop it off at the schools in Antioch. I did just that, and the following week, I received a call from the Principal's secretary to set up a meeting. I couldn't believe it! All I was thinking was, is it possible that we were on our way to another school district?

I met with the Principal, and he loved me, the data and all the great things that my current Principal had to say about me. After jumping through hoops, we were in. Just like that. We were now in another high school running our program. Had my contract never been cut in half at Pittsburg, I wouldn't have gone to drop those packets off, and if I hadn't dropped those packets off, I wouldn't be in the Antioch Unified School District. I didn't have any doors closing; they were shifting, and I loved the way they moved. I was on a magical rollercoaster ride. It was like I was riding something at Disneyland. God was really showing up and showing out.

We started our new school in the middle of the 2016 school year. This was so good because now our finances were growing, and we should be okay for the summer, especially since it seems that we wouldn't get our summer school contract either. With the summer school contract, we wouldn't fall behind on our bills or rent. I didn't know what we were going to do. I was so confused as to what God was doing. Though my back was against the wall, I kept my faith. I prayed for direction, and He gave it to me. I asked for financial freedom, and He was slowly making that happen. I prayed for an increase, and here it was. He decreased us in one area and increased us in another. It's easy for me to keep the faith, as God has put me through so many tests, lessons and obstacles over the years that I know not ever to question or doubt him. He has made a way for me and my family when there was no other way. He saved me from myself and trusted me with students to be their advocate. I knew that He wouldn't forsake me. I was on a mission for him and his people.

We got into Deer Valley High School and did a great job. The mediation counselor had to leave school for a month because of a family emergency, so since we were doing so well, they asked if we could increase our days from two to four, and they would work the contract out later. This was so unreal. I couldn't believe it! Not only was this more days, but once again, this was the blessing we needed. I was so happy. God was playing favorites once again. He knew that even though I had faith, I was scared. This increase was above and beyond our expectations at the time, and we didn't expect this increase. This was double what our initial amount was. In our mind, we were making enough to cover the loss that we would have in the upcoming school year, but we had exceeded what we were making in the Pittsburg Unified School District. This was a dream come true.

Since we were finally doing good financially, we decided to take our kids on a vacation for spring break. We went to Disneyland, Magic Mountain, and then drove all the way to Reno to spend the night at Circus Circus. The kids had a great time, and so did we. We hadn't been able to do something like this since my hustling days. Not only was I making more money than I was when I was hustling, but I had peace of mind. I was no longer stressed, looking over my shoulder, scared when the doorbell rang, thinking it might be the police, and I didn't have to question where my next dollar was going to come from. Because now it was coming every two weeks from multiple sources. We were now in three schools, and the program that everyone said wasn't possible, God made possible. After our first year in Antioch, we spoke with the Principal to see what his thoughts were on us expanding our program to other schools. He was for it, and he even wrote us a letter of recommendation.

The following year, I went to Dallas Ranch Middle School, had a meeting with the VP, which was followed by a meeting with the Principal and just like that, we were in. Trusting the process was all I could do. What we were trying to do in Pittsburg was happening in Antioch. I'm so thankful for this growth, and I praise God every day for trusting me, giving me a great team and never allowing any weapon that forms against us to prosper. The schools are doing good. We've hired more employees, and now I have more free time than I did before, so I'm able to put more time into my writing. This book was inspired by all of the young ladies I work with and counsel. I can see myself in them. I could start and tell my story, but I never knew where I was going in the middle to give it an ending.

I've probably started over five books over the years, and then out of nowhere came the vision for the perfect concept; the book would be a bunch of unique stories. This way, I didn't have to worry about getting stuck in the middle. It was short and sweet. I had Ms. Jenkins and my cousin, Ah-nee' helping me with the edits. My mentor, DB Bedford, gave me the game on how to self-publish and then boom just like that, I was a self-published author! This was unreal. I knew I could write, and I enjoyed doing so. I also knew that I wasn't that good with English. I mispronounce words, don't know where all the punctuation marks go, and I didn't know when to use the right; your, you're, where, were, we're, to, too, two and so on. This was a struggle for me and made my confidence level go down when I thought about becoming an author. Writing comes easy to me, telling stories comes easy, and creating scenarios comes easy. I used to think that in order to write a book, it had to be perfect, it cost a lot, and I needed a publisher. None of this is true. My mentor told me how to self-publish my own books, and I haven't stopped since. My books haven't become the best seller yet, but I know that the stories I tell and the advice I give will help most people that are reading this. I believe this and have faith in this because I believe that this book was written with God leading the way.

I've had a vision for many books, I started about two books

before this book, and yet this book was finished in a month. You will know when you're doing the right thing and when to go after the next new opportunity. Your purpose isn't fulfilled overnight. You can get the vision overnight, and then the obstacles come along, but you have to trust the process. God is always with you. At times, He's testing you and making sure you're prepared for what's ahead. He will make you strong in the areas where you are weak and, at that moment, it might feel like it's too difficult, and you can't handle it. Don't give up because God hasn't given up on you. God's plans aren't always our plans. In order for you to be the best version of you, He has to pull that fear, doubt and anxiety out of you. Open your mind to everything that's happening around you and know that it's not happening to you, but for you, for the greater good of your strength and purpose moving forward.

It's never personal and always purpose, so trust the process and enjoy the marathon because you've already won first place. If you run a race that's not yours, the competition will always have you feeling like you lost. Don't worry about keeping up with them; keep up with your own private thoughts. This way, your vision will stay clear along the way. I'm so honored that God has trusted me with the gift to help, serve and lead people to purpose the way he leads me. You know where I started, and he has taken me from nothing to something. I wasn't doing anything productive or worthwhile when I was in the streets; it was all about me. Now he has trusted me to be the problem solver for young people dealing with a lot of the same traumas and residual social-emotional issues I had dealt with. My journey has been a dream. I have been through so much, and I know that others have gone through more. Even so, I never would have thought that I would be a youth advocate, author, entrepreneur, wife, inspirational speaker, coach, and leader. God has given me the most amazing gift in the world, the gift of voice.

Before, I used my voice in the wrong way. I was using my leadership talents to lead people into doing wrong, doing things that went with my lifestyle. Now I use my voice to inspire, help, support, and motivate people all around the world to do what is right, to fulfill their purpose. The adversity was stressful, and sometimes, I felt like giving up, but with God giving me the strength, I learned to live past the moment. Don't let the moment get you down. Today might be good, tomorrow even better, but there will come the days that make you throw in the towel. I wanted to throw in the towel many times, as soon as I felt that negative thinking coming on. I soon replace it with all the things that I should be thankful for. Not only was I able to start a nonprofit with the best team ever; I was now starting my new business. This business was more about me speaking, coaching and doing workshops.

I've been at this for a few months now, sending emails, making calls, and I even invested a few thousand dollars and still haven't earned $1. I was getting discouraged and was ready to give up. I knew this wasn't an option, and so did my Spirit, so at that moment, I made a promise to myself, and this is what you should do as well. Celebrate every good moment, cherish the phone calls you made, the letters or emails you sent out, the response you received from one of the businesses out of the two hundred you sent out, the call that was returned. Don't be frustrated, be filled with joy, relishing in the memories you will have forever. This is what trusting the process is all about. Trusting the process may cause you to feel stuck, incomplete, or lost because you've invested so much money, time and energy. If you allow yourself to feel this way while waiting until you get that big break you've been waiting for, you might be whiling to quit. You will miss that feeling that comes when the reward pays off upon harvest. The feelings of joy, which is important to experience daily. It gives you the inspiration you need to be resilient. Enjoy every step, trust your vision, listen to your conscious mind, and fear nothing. God is with you every step of the way. Let go of the things and people that you know are holding you back and stop doing the things that cause you more harm than good. Remember, all money ain't good money Listen to your gut feeling, stop running to people, and run to God. Your journey is promised, so don't give up on yourself, and no matter what you go through, always remember, it's Never Personal, Always Purpose.

POEM

My kids give me life

I can't imagine being away from them because of prison another night

God has shown me the light

Living in happiness used to be a challenge

Now that I have God, I feel really lavish

I'm so glad I learned that I don't have to compete

The lord is my Savior; I am saved

I will always give him the Praise

By: Monique Turner

Chapter 7
Power of Purpose

I'm honored that God has shown me a better way of living. He has saved, loved, comforted, guided, and supported me through all life's adversities. I know I have said this many times throughout this book. Without him, none of this would have been possible. The life I live now would still be a dream instead of reality. I took you on a journey with me, from my past to my present, and I opened myself up. To be honest, this was scary for me, to be so honest about things that I've just discovered myself. You might be thinking, how have I just discovered these things when I'm the only one that's been living my life? The thing is, even though you are the only person that can live your life, you have a bunch of people, and other outside influences, guiding you along the way. See, our parents, siblings, family members, teachers, mentors, grandparents, and neighborhood have a huge influence on your life growing up as well as the overall community/environment you grew up in. If you were anything like me, you looked up to the adults in your life, regardless of what they were doing. Their wrong looked right, and their right looked good.

I'm a believer that when you're a child, you start off living your purpose. This is something that I just discovered, based on some of the things I've discovered in examining my past and present. When I was young, free-spirited, not worried about anybody's opinion of me and what I was doing, I was living my best life, my purpose. I was a little girl helping the kids in my community develop an appreciation for education by playing school all the time. Starting a hamburger house at nine years old with my mom was my way of showing my entrepreneurial skills. Being the captain when we played sports showed my leadership skills, and then came all the skills of fitting into the neighborhood that sent me down the wrong path instead of continuing to lead me one step closer to God's promise. I'm taking you back because it's really important for you to know that without going back, you can't go forward. I tried to go forward so many times in my life, and every time, I stayed right where I was or made things worse by chasing money instead of my purpose. Just think about when I told you I got the vision in 2010. I was so focused on starting the nonprofit, but the problem was that I felt I could start a nonprofit being halfway in the streets and the other half of my time trying to do right. God showed me that it doesn't mean that I will live the dream just because I have a vision. I had a lot of cleaning up to do mentally, physically and emotionally.

I always think back to when I was fired from my stationary engineering job for giving the wrong social security. It reminds me of how God showed Moses the land and told him that it would be his when he was ready. I held on to that message for years, knowing that God was speaking to me through T.D. Jakes. Some might think that this is silly, maybe a little presumptuous to compare my situation to that of Moses, but it has come true for me as it did for him. It took me three years to buckle down and say enough is enough of trying to juggle living a double life. I can't dip in and dip out when I want to; I have to be all the way in if I want to receive the blessings that I know God is trying to give me. God never gives up on you, but the path you chose is what determines the outcome. Listen to that quiet voice in your head and don't second guess yourself. Be bold and go for it.

This is the mindset I had once I gave up involvement in illegal activities. I was on a mission and was determined to let nothing stop me. Every time I felt threatened by someone, I would always say to myself, "it is written. No weapon formed against me shall prosper, and every tongue that shall condemn." (Isaiah 54:17) I held on to this, along with a bunch of other scriptures, every day. This is how I maintain my peace, elevating every year, and choosing God's plan over my own. His plan comes with much sacrifice, no understanding, miracles, heartbreak, loneliness, despair, love, guidance, peace, hope, and purpose. When all I could do was feel sorry for myself for losing my parents, going to jail, being cheated on, violated, beat, and being a lost soul, my life was on a roller coaster ride that did more flips and turns than anyone's stomach could handle. This was my normal ride, and I didn't feel like I needed to get off until God gave me the very thing that I envisioned, Family Purpose Organization.

December 2013 was the beginning of my new life. It was unspeakable how God just handed me something that is so sought after. Here it was, me a girl from the hood having my visions come to pass. I never gave up on the dream, and even though I stopped working on it at times, I never gave up on the vision. I just put it on the back burner, and every time I did, it was for the wrong reason, money. I'm so grateful that God took me on a journey, testing my faith and love for money before he started letting me live my purpose 100%. When I first got permission to work in the high school, as I stated in a previous chapter, I had to volunteer for the first six months. This was God testing me to see if I would give up the illegal hustling when my back was against the wall. I was living off my wife and her salary, something I've never done in my life. I've always been able to take care of me. My pride was so strong that it was causing problems whenever she had to take care of our kids and me.

When I was volunteering, we faced so much opposition. Limited finances meant that we couldn't go on any family trips, out to eat, or on a date. We used to go to LA and Vegas at least twice a year. During this phase in our lives, things were tight, and my faith in God was being tested. He needed to know that I could trust him to supply all that we needed and not so dependent on the things that we wanted. I had to trust that he let me in the school to win, not to fail, and he wouldn't forsake me. I was doing something that many who own a 501.C3 organization try to do every day, partner with organizations, and run programs that support their passion. Getting permission to work in the schools is a challenge. Organizations approach the schools every day, and most can't get in. I was successful because of the purpose. It's all about the purpose and God's plan for my life and the life of those I encounter. Being in the schools has opened up so many doors for me; it has really allowed me to be clear on what God wants me to do.

I work with my students, teachers, administrators and principals, in efforts to find a solution to the issues that present themselves as roadblocks. This is part of the reason I know that being a coach is my calling. God wants me to speak to his children, spread his word, and save his people. Once I'd written my first book, it helped to bring back my passion for writing, as I began discovering more about myself and the things I went through in the past. When life gives you ice, you have to know it's going to make water. Things won't be hard forever; there will come a time when what was hard and complicated becomes smooth and easy. You know why? Because God makes everything possible when your actions are aligned with your purpose. When you're in the middle of the storm, trust that the rainbow is coming. So many people waste time worrying more about the storm than the rainbow ahead. Don't get caught up in the moment. Know that what you're working on was meant to be built over a lifetime. Don't settle for short cuts. Do it right, put in the work, stay up late nights, and stay working. It's okay if you don't understand it. Know that your dreams, passion, gifts, and talents were planted within you by God. Don't get caught up in the adversity that's trying to slow you down. Stay in the race because it's your race and you've already won. Let the Marathon continue...

Running the nonprofit and working with my students has changed me. They have helped me know who I am. My kids know the real me. It's funny how you can be honest with kids and have to wear a mask with adults. Some people are scared to live their truth, based on their past or present life experiences. Society will have you feeling that you're not good enough if you're not like everyone you see on TV. But here's the thing, trying to do what you see everyone else doing won't allow you to step into your purpose. I remember when I was younger, I wanted to dress like the rappers I saw on TV, Jay-Z, T.I, DMX, and TLC. I wanted my style to be just like theirs. Not only did I buy the same clothes they were wearing, I even wore my clothes the way they did. Sweatsuits and Timberlands were my style. I wish I were trying to be more like me back then, as who knew where that might have brought me.

Living on purpose comes with many responsibilities because as it is written, "to much is given much is required" (Luke 12:48). I'm still learning this. I pray for so much because I want to be on a different level. I want to be able to provide more, but like they say, more money, more problems. These are true statements from what I see so far. God doesn't give me what I pray for when I pray for it. He supplies me with what I need to serve his people and not what I want for my own personal needs. This used to bother me and was part of the reason why I would get up and make things happen on my own. But waiting on him keeps me from making mistake after mistake. I've learned that letting go and letting God allows me to keep my peace of mind.

I chased money for so long; it was all that I knew and being without it wasn't an option. You need money to live. Having spent all my life hustling, when I came home from prison, you see you can have it all, but when you get locked up, all that you had can become a distant memory, especially if you didn't get a chance to get things in order before you go. I was blessed that God let me bail out to fight my case from the streets before I was sentenced. I was able to get my son and living situation in order before I went to serve my five years in federal prison. God had me then, and I wasn't seeking him; He was the last person on my list at that time. My grief at losing my parents and the thought of going to prison wouldn't let me call on him. The blessing behind that is that God doesn't wait on us; He saves us. Once I came home, and He saw that I was still with the street movement, He broke me all the way down, making sure I trusted him and put all my faith in him for all things, especially when it came to money.

I remember going to my little sister to borrow money because I didn't like having to ask my wife for money when she would get paid. This was during my time of battling between the legal and illegal hustle. My sister wasn't the only person that I borrowed money from. I remember needing to borrow money from my auntie so that I could pay for my tools for work when I was a cement mason. But why did I borrow money instead of getting it from my wife? This made no sense, especially since it was being spent with her. At one point, I even had a gambling addiction because I was so busy chasing money. This almost ruined my marriage; I was spending more money than I was making. I was so busy trying to get that quick come up that I wasn't seeing the problems I was causing my family financially.

I would spend my last money on gambling, and when we would go to Vegas, I would be in the Casino until the sun came up. My wife would be furious with me. When we would be with a group of people, she would be okay, but when it was just the two of us, she would leave me sometimes. Most of the time, this would ruin our trip because all I wanted to do was gamble and all she wanted to do was shop. At the time, I didn't care because, in my mind, I would go get it back in the streets. I even borrowed money from my Twin. I didn't need the money for bills; I needed the money to hang out on the weekend. The cold part is it took me forever to pay it back, not because I didn't have it, but I was too busy spending it trying to get a quick come up. It's sad when I look back and analyze just how the devil had my mind; he was controlling me. I was never going to win like that; I would have continued to lose.

I stopped gambling, and I've been winning ever since. I can go to Vegas now and walk right past the machines and tables. Before, I had to stop in every Casino just to try my luck. Money hadn't done anything but cause me problems when I was focused on it and not the purpose. I praise God that He saved me from my love of money. Now, I work hard for the purpose and not the money. The funny thing about that is, I make more money now than I've ever made in the streets hustling or anywhere else. It's beyond amazing what can happen when you find your purpose and really begin to activate it, never quitting and never looking back.

Let me take you on this quick time zone with me. I want you to really understand what life has been like for me since I found my purpose. I gave you the stories leading up to the purpose, but just because I'm living it doesn't mean that it's easy. I'm so grateful for the Family Purpose Organization; I'm honored that God trusted me to help youth deal with their social-emotional issues. I've been blessed to partner with multiple districts throughout East County and partner with multiple schools, implementing our programs. We have been fortunate enough to partner with the county to run workshops with foster youth on social media etiquette and tobacco prevention. None of this would be possible without God. I know you know, especially after reading the book, that I believe with everything in me, that God is the key to finding your purpose and living it. Once again, God was playing favorites with me. In 2014, my record was expunged, in 2015, we were in two schools, three schools in 2016, four schools in 2017, five schools in 2018 in and now 2019, we have run workshops in over eight schools.

The thing about purpose is, it never stops. There's always something to be done. The nonprofit was the beginning to the promise ahead. In 2017, I wrote my first book on social media etiquette. This book is the blueprint to help people see that social media can be a very deceptive, volatile, and dynamic communication medium, and you shouldn't take what someone posts personally. I received the vision to write this book from my students. Listening to them day after day allowed me to see that they have very few to relate to. I see myself in them, so I believed that pieces of my story might help. In 2018, we were blessed with two contracts at the first school to give us an opportunity to manifest change within the school system. That school was Pittsburg High. Through our hard work, dedication and God's grace, we finally received a contract for our college track program, Academics, Accountability and Advocacy. The AAA program helps prepare participants for the next level, and even though we've been running this program for free, we have finally been blessed with a contract.

In addition, we have a contract for our Successful Purpose program, which helps students deal with their social-emotional issues. This was actually the first program I designed. I didn't let my lack of confidence keep me from jumping right in. I knew how to run a program; I'd been doing it since I was a child. Successful Purpose was more my speed because of all the social-emotional issues I endured as a child. The AAA program was run by Ms. Ah-nee', our cousin, who is super smart. She graduated high school with her AA and went to UC Davis and graduated at 19 years old. She was perfect for our students. Then there was my wife Tiffany and Ms. Jenkins, who started the program. They all worked on this program together to bring it to life. This was all God. He was sending me who I needed when I needed them. All I had to do was pray and be patient in waiting on him. I would always pray for him to send me the right people to take this organization to the next level, and he did just that.

I hired a young lady, who had been out of high school for two years, who wanted to do this type of work because she was once a troubled teen. She did great work with us for about a year, and after that, she fell off. I had to understand that just like I wasn't ready at first, neither was she. I'm just glad that I was able to give her a chance to live her dream for the moment. I know God put her in my path to mentor her, and when she comes back, I will be right here with open arms to help her find her passion again. It's funny because in the midst of writing this book, she has come back to work with us. I could have rejected her, but where is the purpose in that? I know that she was sent from God, and God wants me to help guide her. The process won't be a fairy tale, it will be life and testimony we will both be able to share with many. God shows up for us, and we must show up for his people.

I know that God puts me in people's paths for a reason and a season; sometimes, I can recognize it; sometimes, I miss it. I didn't do anything special to be a person that God uses. All I did was trust, believe, and have faith in him. What a blessing that has been bestowed upon us. We now have two programs in the school we started volunteering at. We began with one day, increased each year to make five days, then decreased to three days, for budgetary reasons. This was a bit disheartening but look at how God works? Our time in one school was decreased so that we could increase our time and services at another school site. There's so much power in purpose, and God has been showing me that since I opened my mind to receive him. I could've given up hope, lost faith when we got hit with fewer days, but instead, I turned that opposition into opportunities. Every year, the number of schools increase, and so do our days.

Principals have told me how they get over five organizations a day trying to get into their schools. I know this is true because sometimes, I'm one of those five. Just like now, I went to a few new middle schools to see about having our program at their school. I haven't heard back from them, but do you think that's going to stop me? It's actually going to do the opposite. I'm going to send another email tomorrow, call the next day and then pop up on Friday. You have to be persistent when you want something, and if it doesn't happen after you've given it your all, then you know for a fact that it's not for you at this time. That doesn't mean it won't be for you at a later date. The key is to never give up, never sell yourself short, and never settle for what looks good at that moment. Making a permanent decision in a temporary situation can make the process longer.

Every day, I pray for God to make my purpose clear. I know that I'm living it, but I still feel incomplete. I know that it doesn't stop with the nonprofit or the book I wrote. The more I pray, the more it becomes clear that He wants me to speak his word. When I heard that, I couldn't believe it. This shouldn't have been a big shock to me since that's all I'd been doing the past few years; everything that comes out my mouth has God in it. Most of my friends call me Pastor Mo, Doctor Mo, or consider me their therapist. I had created a Facebook group #iAmHer. This group was designed to provide women with a platform to discuss the daily issues we face. As things progressed, that group soon morphed into #OurSpiritualJourney.

This was inspired by a daily devotional book I ordered online. I started to post the current day in the group, and the ladies loved it. Everyone would always thank me and say how much they appreciated me posting it. I did this from March 2017, the day I received the book, until March 2018. Sometimes, I would post the wrong month, I would post April, and it was May. I felt that everyone was missing the message, myself included, but I wanted us all to get it. So, I decided to write a 90-Day Spiritual Journey Book for myself and my audience. This book was going to be different from any other daily devotional book written. It was a process getting it right, but I'm honored to say that in October 2018, I self-published my second book. I couldn't believe it. I had written two books. Both books were different; they had the same model using the #iAmHer, but everything else was different. What they did have in common was they were both filled with advice and tools on how to address situations from a different perspective. I was doing what God wanted me to do. I was following my visions, planting seeds and watching them grow to see the harvest.

If it weren't for my amazing team: my wife, Smoothie, Ahnee', and Ms. Jenkins, along with the staff members that we've hired over time, none of this would've been possible. See, teamwork makes the dream work, and without the team, I wouldn't be telling the story. It doesn't matter that the visions were mine. I'm just the one that God is using to speak through. He's trusted me to lead his people into the promised land. So, now that I have these books, I want to make sure that I advertise and market the organization.

Part of that was creating our own T-shirt printing business, designing and selling clothing that represented what we stood for. We started the company with Ms. Jenkins. Instead of paying for my shirts to be made, Ms. Jenkins would use her machine, and we're able to do them ourselves. This was good because it allowed us to use the money we made from the shirts and put it back into the program. This was perfect because it reduced our out of pocket costs and paid for some of the things that we do with our students.

We've been blessed to sponsor 10 students for the prom, provide sashes on graduation day for all our seniors, parties celebrating our honor roll students, field trips, college scholarships, and more. We've been very blessed to be able to do all this without any private funders, grants or angel investors. This past year, we set up a donation link on Facebook for anyone who wanted to donate to our prom sponsorship, and we raised $1,000. This was the first time besides the $2,500 grant we received in 2013 from Keller Canyon. We work hard every day to support our youth, but this was money given to us in recognition of all that we do, and we are forever grateful for acknowledgement like this. Now, comes the vision to start an LLC. In doing this, I can separate my books, shirts, and coaching from the nonprofit. Again, I began to question myself.

How am I supposed to start a business? I don't know anything about starting a business. Who's going to help me? Where would I find the money to begin this business? Most of the money that was coming in is being absorbed by the costs of running our nonprofit. These are all the thoughts going through my mind, but I had to trust God. My friend, Unicorn, connected me with the right people to get the ball rolling, and again, just like that, I had an LLC, Family Purpose Enterprises. I had to wait a few months to pay the corporate lawyer because I was living paycheck to paycheck. When you're focused on the purpose, nothing else matters. You are willing to do what needs to be done to see it through, despite the slow movement and financial limitations. You keep going and never give up.

You appreciate the small accomplishments and cherish each step moving forward. Despite the adversity I faced, I always kept moving towards living my purpose. Family Purpose Enterprises LLC was formed in March 2018. I was clueless about what this business would do; I just knew I needed a business to follow the nonprofit because you can't make money off a nonprofit. With a nonprofit, you give more then you make. Plus, to build the community center for Family Purpose, I need my income to increase. I can't sit around and expect someone to give us a location. I've already tried asking for a space from the city of Pittsburg, and they said they didn't have any locations that they could sponsor us with. So, I needed to make this happen. I knew this, and so did God. I started a Facebook like page and began posting my motivational quotes and videos. This was a way for me to gain the attention that I needed for more people to know what I'm doing. My motto was no matter what happens to us in this life; we must always remember that it's "never personal...always purpose."

Then came the vision to turn Never Personal Always Purpose, into an LLC. I needed to build my brand, and the only way I was truly going to do this was to have everything under the same name. I thought that Family Purpose Enterprises was it, but what I was talking about and the books I was writing didn't fit with that name. A few years back, I came up with the saying Never Personal, Always Purpose. Saying this to myself would keep me level. This would keep me at peace and focused on the promise ahead instead of my current situation. See, when you doubt yourself and lack confidence, you're more likely to take constructive criticism personally. That is what I used to do all that time. I hated for someone to tell me about me. I didn't want to hear it; I thought I knew it all, but the truth was, even though I seemed to be very confident, it was something I lacked. If I wanted to have all that God was trying to give me; I needed to get out my own way. This was something that I had to learn to master if I was going to succeed with all the odds against me.

I started Never Personal, Always Purpose LLC in April 2018. At this point, it started to feel like everything was coming together, and I was further along my path in speaking and spreading the word of God. I still don't know to what capacity he wants me to spread the good news. I feel that he wants me to do it in my own unique way. Though my story is not unique, the platform from which I am speaking and the ways in which I am communicating are. My lifestyle and the experiences that I have had have allowed me to show people the power of their voice. I am in a same-sex marriage, which many believe is already against what the Bible has written...the funny thing about that to me is, God came into my life and saved me once I started having same-sex relationships.

Everyone has their own perspective on what the Bible means to them. Pastors take scripture and interpret the word to fit their sermon of the day. Who's to say that their understanding of the scripture is the correct or only way to interpret it? I've learned that for me to really trust God, I had to build my own relationship with him and not base it off what my pastor or anybody else thinks. A lot has been written that many follow and a lot that many don't follow. I chose to follow God, Jesus and the holy spirit, moving forward, knowing that God is love, love thy neighbor and fear nobody but God. This is what I follow and, in doing so, not only have I discovered my peace, I've discovered my purpose, and now I'm living it.

It's now November 2018, and I haven't gotten a single client, lead or earned one dollar from NPAP, yet. But knowing what it's going to prosper into because of the seeds that I'm planting now is all a dream come true. Over the past few months, I've been paying for ads, making a bunch of posts each day, and trying to build new connections that can help me expand. My goal is to speak the word of God all around the world, spreading the good news, and changing people's perspective on the power of purpose.

In October 2018, I got the vision to write this book, The NPAP Blueprint. I felt I needed to write this book to give people the blueprint that led me to my purpose, in hopes it will bless all my readers to search for their purpose. Even though I share my story on social sites, this book was different because it was my full truth, the tools needed to never give up. Every day, I'm living my purpose, regardless of the pressure, adversity, opposition or fear that I might face. I know that I must press if this is what I want. I could have stopped with the nonprofit, instead of hiring people to run each school, figuring the team, and I could do it, but when you're living on purpose, you step out of your comfort zone day after day. I'm like a little kid running around a candy store. I'm all over the place and don't know what to do next.

All I have is my visions from God, his direction, and that's all I need. When you're living on purpose, your direction comes from the Lord and being still is the only way to hear him. When I don't feel progress within, I pray and ask God to direct me. Everything I have has been fruits of my visions from God. It's mind-blowing to see how far I've come and to know how far I'm going, all from a vision. This just goes to show how God chooses us for his purpose. Not because you have an expensive house or car, but because you are you, a soul worth saving. I didn't seek God; He came seeking me.

He sent my friend into my room because I was grieving wrong behind my dad. I was lost, sad, lonely, feeling despair, and He knew I needed him.

God knew that without him, I wouldn't transform into the woman I am today. He picked me to comfort, save, love, coach, lead, guide and inspire lost souls just as I was in the past. He blessed me to show everyone that living on purpose isn't about how much money you have; it's about being at peace within and doing what God created you to do. I'm living my purpose, but the work I'm doing is far from done. I know that I'm on a lifetime assignment for the Lord. My advice to you is, don't sit down, stand up, be bold, be courageous, and believe in you. Don't be scared to jump; God will catch you. If you continue to play it safe, you will never step into your purpose, reaching your destiny. Everything about living on purpose is unfamiliar and uncomfortable in the beginning and, as soon as you have it, here comes God with another curveball. That curveball isn't for you to strike out; it's for you to hit a grand slam.

If it's something you don't know, research it; do what you have to do in order to accomplish the mission God has you on. Use this when you're scared of what their response might be when you're asking for something. The worst they can do is say, "No." Whenever you are feeling uncertain, tell yourself, "God has me in a position of power. Why should I be scared or nervous when God has placed me in this position?" I had to learn that doubting myself, feeling like I was unqualified, or less than, wasn't an option anymore. Whenever I found myself feeling this way, I would remember what the scripture says, "So do not fear, for I am with you; do not be dismayed, for I am your God. I will strengthen you and help you" (Isaiah 41:10). I know this and believe this because of the many miracles that I've seen God perform, saving me from myself and others.

Trust me; it's scary to give up everything and step out of faith. Many people never find their purpose because they are scared to get out their comfort zone. Think about how many people get up every day and go to work unhappy, day after day and year after year because they need the pay, benefits or retirement package. They wake up miserable, and they make the people at their job miserable. They get mad and jealous of the people they know that did what they couldn't do. I praise God for my wife; she really made it easy for me to walk out on faith, bringing my visions to life. I know that if God hadn't sent her to me, none of this would have been possible. That's why I pray that God blesses me to take care of my wife and family for generations to come. Even if you don't have that special someone to hold you down while you walk out on faith, think about what is in your power to actualize your dreams. It's all about baby steps. Maybe, you can work your 9 to 5 job and still put in a few hours a day working on your passion. Whatever you do, stop waiting on THEM or MONEY. You must listen to God, knowing that you aren't perfect, and you will make mistakes. You will do something today that won't truly manifest until a year later.

Most of the amazing things happening for me now are from seeds that I've planted years ago. It's all about trusting the process. You have to be your number one cheerleader and avoid the chatter when it's negative. Celebrate the positive. I celebrate every accomplishment like I've won an Oscar. Doing this keeps me excited, and you want to stay excited. This, in turn, will help you stay encouraged. I want you to hold on to this every day as you embrace your purpose. No matter what they do, say, or how they feel about what you're doing, It's Never Personal, Always Purpose. Remember this, live it, and apply it to your thinking process. I know that it will help you continue to move forward with all odds against you. This next scripture is a scripture that I've memorized to keep me from going off on people and bringing the old Monique out. This scripture gives me peace and faith in God for all things.

As it is written:

(Psalm 23)

The Lord is my Shepherd, to feed, to guide and to shield me, I shall not want. 2. He lets me lie down in green pastures: he leads me beside the still and quiet waters. 3. He refreshes and restores my soul (life). He leads me in the paths of righteousness for his name sake. 4. Even though I walk through the (sunless) valley of the shadow of death, I fear no evil, for you and with me, your rod (to protect) and your staff (to guide), they comfort and console me. 5. You prepare a table before me in the presence of my enemies. You have anointed and refreshed my head with oil: my cup overflows. 6. Surely goodness and mercy and unfailing love shall follow me all the days of my life, and I shall dwell forever (throughout all my days) in the house and in the presence of the Lord.

I'm going to break this scripture down for you and show you how I've been able to apply it to my life and how it's helped me to continue to live my purpose each day. Verse 1; knowing I have

God to feed, guide and shield me. Knowing this gives me the courage I need to walk out on faith, especially if I really trust God's word, and why wouldn't I trust God's word? I've trusted the word of a fool, so why not the man that created us. Verse 2; He leads me to quiet waters, not chaos or trouble, but to peace. Everything in this book shows how he leads us from the chaos and trouble; He changed my life. Verse 3; He's the reason I have these visions and He's leading me to righteousness if I let him, and it's all about him getting the glory. Verse 4; Even though I've sinned my whole life, never seeking him and doing things the way of the flesh, I can trust him, I will fear no evil, knowing that God is with me. Verse 5; Every time I thought I wasn't good enough, fearing the people in the schools with higher power who doubted me, He prepared a table in their presence making me powerful, a force to be noticed. Verse 6; Because I gave up my old life, walked out on faith, fearing nobody but God, I know that his grace, mercy and goodness will follow me all the days of my life.

It's scripture like this that has allowed me to put my faith in God, not just because of what it reads, but because of how I can see this very scripture being applied to my life. Scripture can pull you out from feeling depressed or anxiety if you're willing to get out of your comfort zone and try a new approach. It's helped me in those areas. Even if you've been in a church your whole life, you can gain a new perspective hearing from someone new. What used to work might not work for you anymore; don't stay stuck, think about the changes you need to make. What does it cost you to try some-thing new? What does it cost you to change the way you think? Since it doesn't cost you anything, why not do it? Because then you have the question, What can you gain if you try something new? How good would you feel seeing new results? I want you to write these questions down and answer them. Then I want you to begin applying action to all the things you're most passionate about, so you can begin living your purpose. Trust the process, and let God guide you one step closer to living your purpose.

The enemy will always show up; you have to be disciplined. God is the key to peace; He is the key to living the life that you were created to live. Release the past, rediscover your passions, and get fired up on your journey of purpose.

POEM

Giving God the Glory

When you gave me my first vision, I didn't know I would write this story

I'm grateful you never leave me; you're with me every step of the way

You guide me to greatness, even when I want to sit and play

Many doubted what I would be able to do and say

The way that we're moving, I'm headed to owning my own shoe

I am past the part of doubting you

Nobody knows the struggles I've gone through

Trust the Process; this is what I'm showing you

When God opens doors, you know it is for you

ABOUT THE AUTHOR

Monique Turner is a businesswoman, youth advocate, and author. As a child, Turner was very social and carried her ability to network and empathize with others into adulthood. Her debut book, #iAm-Her, was inspired by conversations she had with women, which proved to be a testimony to the connectedness we all have. She is the founder and Executive Director of Family Purpose, a not for profit organization dedicated to improving the station of students of color in the school and juvenile justice system. Together with her board of directors, staff and volunteers, Turner is committed to empowering the next generation by providing them with the tools and resources to be the authors of their own stories.

My little sister (Wayzata) and Monique "the Tomboy"

Where it all started. Valencia Gardens: 15 Below or VGs

Club nights with my people from the block.

Prison picture of me

ATTORNEY OR PARTY WITHOUT ATTORNEY (Name, State Bar number, and address):

Monique Turner

ATTORNEY FOR (Name): Monique Turner

PEOPLE OF THE STATE OF CALIFORNIA

v.

DEFENDANT: Monique Turner

FOR COURT USE ONLY

FILED

2014 JAN 21 A 9:37

H. HASH
CLERK OF THE SUPERIOR COURT
COUNTY OF CONTRA COSTA, CA

BY _____ DEPUTY CLERK

PETITION FOR DISMISSAL
(Pen. Code, §§ 17, 1203.4, 1203.4a)

CASE NUMBER:
5121808-0

DEFENDANT'S INFORMATION

DRIVER'S LIC #:

SSN # (LAST FOUR DIGITS ONLY):

DATE OF BIRTH:

1. On (date): _____ the defendant in the above-entitled criminal action was convicted of a violation of section(s) (specify): _____ of the (specify): _____ Code.

2. The offense was a ☐ misdemeanor ☑ felony.
   Felony offense (Pen. Code, § 17):
   ☑ The offense listed above is a felony that may be reduced to a misdemeanor under Penal Code section 17.

3. ☑ Offense with probation granted (Pen. Code, § 1203.4):
   Probation was granted on the terms and conditions set forth in the docket of the above-entitled court; the defendant is not serving a sentence for any offense, nor on probation for any offense, nor under charge of commission of any crime, and the defendant (check one):
   a. ☐ has fulfilled the conditions of probation for the entire period thereof;
   b. ☑ has been discharged from probation prior to the termination of the period thereof; or
   c. ☐ should be granted relief in the interests of justice. (Please note: You must explain why granting a dismissal would be in the interests of justice by completing and attaching the optional Attached Declaration (form MC-031).)

4. ☐ Offense with sentence other than probation (Pen. Code, § 1203.4a):
   ☐ Probation was not granted; more than one year has elapsed since the date of pronouncement of judgment. The defendant has complied with the sentence of the court and is not serving a sentence for any offense nor under charge of commission of any crime, and since said pronouncement of judgment has lived an honest and upright life and conformed to and obeyed the laws of the land.

Petitioner requests that defendant be permitted to withdraw the plea of guilty, or that the verdict or finding of guilt be set aside and a plea of not guilty be entered and the court dismiss this action under section ☒ 1203.4 or ☐ 1203.4a of the Penal Code.

☑ Petitioner requests that the felony charge be reduced to a misdemeanor under Penal Code section 17.

I declare under penalty of perjury under the laws of the State of California that the foregoing is true and correct.

Executed on: January, 21 2014
(DATE)

▶ _____
(SIGNATURE OF PETITIONER OR ATTORNEY)

Petition for dismissal from probation

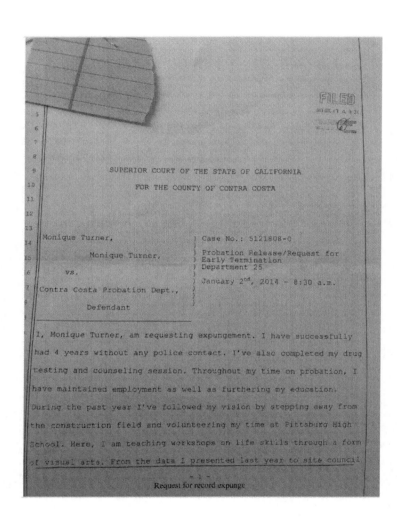

SUPERIOR COURT OF THE STATE OF CALIFORNIA

FOR THE COUNTY OF CONTRA COSTA

Monique Turner,	Case No.: 5121808-0
Monique Turner,	Probation Release/Request for Early Termination Department 25
vs.	January 2nd, 2014 - 8:30 a.m.
Contra Costa Probation Dept.,	
Defendant	

I, Monique Turner, am requesting expungement. I have successfully had 4 years without any police contact. I've also completed my drug testing and counseling session. Throughout my time on probation, I have maintained employment as well as furthering my education. During the past year I've followed my vision by stepping away from the construction field and volunteering my time at Pittsburg High School. Here, I am teaching workshops on life skills through a form of visual arts. From the data I presented last year to site council

- 1 -

Request for record expunge

Motion for dismissal

Pictures of me and my family on outings after prison

Me and my family on vacation to Cabo

My Grandson, Dante and son, Juju

My siblings

HAPPY NEW YEARS FROM THE YOUTH

The Dream Team 2019

Turner Mo

JULY 2, 2018

Camping 2018

My niece and nephew

Vegas with the family 2019

Our family
Butter Sr, Jr. and me

The marathon continues -RIH Nipsey

Chuck E. Cheese with the kids

My family 2014

Me and my wife 2019

My Down South family (Mississippi)

My family

Me as a little girl

The tomboy me, little sister and our cousin

Turner Mo

DECEMBER 15, 2010 🔒

Family Vegas trip

Miami girls' trip

My kids

Grandma and Uncle Tommy

My god-daughter and her family

Our Autie and Cousin

SIL and us

7-day family cruise

Me, my cousin and my brother

My family

My mom and dad

My dad at work

My mom